PARENTAL ALIENATION IS PSYCHOLOGICAL MALTREATMENT

FIRST EDITION

A PRACTICAL, EVIDENCE-BASED GUIDE TO IDENTIFY, DIAGNOSE & CONNECT THE DOTS

CHERYL MEFFERD
BSN, RN

Every effort has been made by the author and publishing house to ensure that the information contained in this book was correct as of press time. The author and publishing house hereby disclaim and do not assume liability for any injury, loss, damage, or disruption caused by errors or omissions, regardless of whether any errors or omissions result from negligence, accident, or any other cause. Readers are encouraged to verify any information contained in this book prior to taking any action on the information.

For rights and permissions, please contact:

Cheryl Mefferd
P.O. Box 1614
Hollister, MO 65673
I'd love to hear how this book has helped you!
Cheryl @ Parental Alienation Speaks.com

The Why

For years, Jack and I watched helplessly as his three amazing children that couldn't wait to come to our home faded into withdrawn, manipulative strangers that would accuse us of things that never happened. It was like watching an avalanche happening in slow motion. *Something* was changing them.

After years of the unknown, we finally had the term- parental alienation. Like so many, we believed that since we had a name, we could stop it from happening. This would prove to be false.

In 2018, I started the blog **Parental Alienation Speaks.com** in an attempt to tell the world our story in bite-sized pieces. Today, that blog is a non-profit organization that not only shares our story but educates mental health professionals, GALs, attorneys, advocates and parents around the world about parental alienation.

On a recent call, an attorney told me she loved my presentation—but she needed more. She needed clarity on how parental alienation qualifies as psychological maltreatment. What diagnoses apply? How do the behaviors fit within clinical frameworks? How can we see and understand this better? I promised her I'd get her the answers. That promise led me to comb through years of notes, research, and insights—and ultimately, that's what became the guide you're holding now.

My goal was to take all of that insight and organize it into something simple, practical, and immediately usable. **This book is built on evidence-based research to help professionals identify, diagnose, and connect the dots between parental alienation and psychological maltreatment.**

These aren't my theories—it's the collective wisdom of countless experts who've dedicated their lives to understanding and exposing this invisible crisis that's tearing families apart and swallowing our children whole.

Almost exactly one year ago from this book's publication, I stood at the funeral of my cousin, Veronica Butler. Her story made national headlines. She was brutally murdered—another life lost because of parental alienation.

I've tried to walk away from this work, to set it down and move on. But the truth is, I can't. It's etched into my life now. And I won't stop—not until childhoods are saved.

So I ask you: Please, share this guide. Give it to advocates, attorneys, mental health professionals, and alienated parents. This isn't about profit—it's about protection. It's about reclaiming stolen childhoods.

Together, we can make a difference!

♡ Cheryl

"Parental alienation (PA) is a serious mental condition that affects hundreds of thousands of children and families in the United States and comparable numbers in other countries. Mental health professionals (MHPs), family law attorneys, and everyday citizens observe PA on a regular basis, even if they do not know that the phenomenon has a name, where it comes from, or what to do about it."

(Lorandos et al., 2013,p. 5)

Table of Contents

Table of Contents

Table of Contents

Table of Contents

Table of Contents

Table of Contents

What is Parental Alienation?

"Parental alienation is the result of an alienating parent's coercion, control and generation of fear in the child toward the targeted parent, making this a very complex form of family violence (as cited in Clawar & Rivlin, 2013; Harman et al., 2018)" (Harman et al., 2019).

"Recent studies have identified parental alienation as a form of family violence that can result in traumatized children being located with an abusive parent who is likely to eventually re-traumatize them" (Roma et al., 2022).

"[Parental alienation]...is typically enacted over time (as cited in Verrocchio, Baker & Marchetti, 2017) and alongside other clusters of behaviors with the intent of hurting, damaging or destroying the child's relationship with that parental figure, and/or to hurt the parental figure themselves" (Harman et al., 2018).

"Parental alienation refers to a psychological condition in which a child allies himself or herself strongly with an alienating (or preferred) parent and rejects a relationship with the alienated (or targeted) parent without legitimate justification (as cited in Lorandos et al, 2013)" (Harman et al., 2019).

Chapter #1: What Is PA?

"Parental alienating behaviors are...both hostile and instrumental forms of aggression" (Harman et al., 2018).

"...no longer a custody issue but a child protection issue" (Boch-Galhau, 2018).

"...very subtle" (Lorandos et al., 2013, p.76).

"...a serious form of family violence" (Harman et al., 2019).

"...the signs and symptoms [of PA] are infinite" (Lorandos et al., 2013, p.76).

"...a specific form of child psychological abuse" (Boch-Galhau, 2018).

"...a complex form of child psychological maltreatment, with significant negative consequences" (Roma et al., 2022).

"Parental alienation is the outcome associated with alienating behaviors (as cited in Baker & Eichler, 2016)" (Harman et al., 2018).

"...a serious form of child emotional abuse associated with physical abuse and neglect" (Roma et al., 2022).

"...psychological maltreatment" (Verrocchio et al., 2018).

"...a form of child psychological abuse" (Boch-Galhau, 2018).

"...an unacknowledged form of family violence" (Harman et al., 2018).

Chapter #1: What Is PA?

4

Chapter #1: What Is PA?

What We Know About PA From Evidence-Based Research...

- **PA affects an estimated 3.5 million children within the US** (Marsden et al., 2024,p.2).
- **It is estimated that about 9% [approx. 30 million] of the US adult population are currently being alienated from their child(ren) by the other parent** (Marsden et al., 2024,p.2).
- **Both mothers & fathers alienate** (Harman et.al, 2019).
- **It occurs in both intact and non-intact families** (Harman et al, 2019).
- **According to research, custodial status, not gender, is typically a predictor of who is likely to alienate** (Harman et al., 2018).
- **Parental alienation does not discriminate. Research shows evidence of parental alienation across all socio-economic and demographic indicators** (Harman et al., 2016).
- **Over half of all PA cases are reported as severe** (Harman et al., 2019).
- **Poor psychological adjustment occurs as a result of PA** (Boch-Galhau, 2018).
- **25% of children from high conflict break-ups will become alienated** (Harman et al., 2016).
- **The strategies to alienate a child are endless** (Boch-Galhau, 2018).
- **Approximately 5-7% of abuse comes to the attention of child protective services (CPS) and psychological abuse goes more unidentified than any other form of abuse** (Pearl, 2015).
- **Research indicates that 47% of moderately to severely alienated parents have contemplated suicide within the past year** (Colorado State University, 2019).
- **A recent study found that 23% of targeted parents reported having attempted suicide** (Lee-Maturana et al., 2020).

Chapter #2: What We Know About PA

DEFINITIONS

The Alienating Parent (AP)

The Alienating Parent (AP), also referred to as the favored parent, is an individual—often a parent or authority figure—who deliberately uses manipulation, coercion, and emotional abuse to damage or destroy the child's relationship with the other parent, commonly known as the Target Parent (TP) (Harman et al., 2018).

Key Traits and Personality Types of an Alienating Parent

- **Narcissistic Personality Traits**
  - Displays an excessive need for admiration and validation.
  - Lacks empathy for the child's emotional distress.
  - Alienating parents frequently demonstrate narcissistic tendencies, such as an inflated sense of self-importance and a belief that they are the only suitable parent for the child (Harman et al, 2019).
- **Borderline Personality Traits**
  - Exhibits intense emotional instability, black-and-white thinking.
  - Fear of abandonment leads them to weaponize the child's emotions.
  - Certain alienating parents display traits associated with borderline personality disorder, relying on the child for emotional stability while persistently casting the other parent in a negative and adversarial role (Baker & Darnall, 2006).
- **Paranoid Personality Traits**
  - Holds extreme, unjustified distrust toward the target parent.

- Convinces the child that the TP is dangerous or untrustworthy.
  - Paranoid alienating parents frequently portray themselves as victims while leading the child to believe that the targeted parent poses a danger (Harman et al., 2018).
- **Sociopathic Traits**
  - Manipulative, deceitful, and willing to lie about the TP to control the child.
  - Lacks remorse for the psychological harm caused to the child.
  - Some alienating parents demonstrate sociopathic traits, employing manipulation and deceit to guarantee the child's rejection of the targeted parent (Harman et al, 2018).

Chapter #3: Definitions

The Target Parent (TP)

The **Target Parent (TP)** is the parent who is unjustifiably rejected by their child due to the manipulative actions of the alienating parent (AP) (Baker & Verrocchio, 2015; Harman et al., 2018). TPs often experience profound emotional, legal, and psychological distress as they struggle to maintain a relationship with their child despite the alienating tactics employed by the AP.

Characteristics and Experiences of a Target Parent:

- **Endure Unwarranted Rejection**
    - The TP is often perceived by the child as unworthy of love, despite no history of abuse or neglect (Harman et al., 2018).
    - The child's rejection is not based on personal experiences but on the negative narratives constructed by the AP (Baker & Verrocchio, 2015).
- **Continuously Face a Distorted Perception from the Child**
    - The AP manipulates the child into believing the TP is dangerous, unloving, or unworthy of a relationship (Harman & Biringen, 2016).
    - Children may exhibit "borrowed scenarios"—repeating false allegations or exaggerated stories about the TP, often using adult language or phrases they do not fully understand (Warshak, 2010).
- **Continuously Face Interference with Parenting Time**
    - APs frequently interfere with court-ordered visitation by:
        - Canceling visits at the last minute (Baker & Darnall, 2006).
        - Claiming the child is too ill to see the TP (Baker & Darnall, 2006).

- Convincing the child they have the right to refuse visits, even when legally mandated (Warshak, 2010).
- **Continuously Face False Allegations of Abuse and Neglect**
  - **Weaponization of the Legal System** – Alienating parents exploit false abuse allegations to gain an unfair advantage in custody disputes. False accusations are frequently employed as a strategy to break the bond between the child and the targeted parent, and in some cases, courts prioritize caution, which can lead to serious and unjust outcomes for the accused parent (Lorandos et al., 2013).
  - **Severe Emotional and Psychological Toll** – Target parents experience chronic stress, anxiety, and depression due to ongoing legal battles and character attacks. Being wrongfully accused of abuse can cause severe psychological distress, with symptoms similar to those of post-traumatic stress disorder (Harman et al., 2018).
  - **Restricted or Lost Parenting Time** – False allegations often result in emergency protective orders or supervised visitation, depriving children of a meaningful relationship with the TP. These false accusations are designed to block court-ordered visitation, effectively preventing the targeted parent from maintaining a consistent role in the child's life (Baker & Darnall, 2006).
  - **Manipulation of the Child's Perception** – The AP reinforces the false narrative, causing the child to fear or distrust the TP. Children who are alienated may begin to accept false accusations of abuse as truth because of continuous exposure to the manipulative tactics of the alienating parent (Verrocchio et al., 2018).
  - **Damage to Reputation and Career** – Accusations of abuse and neglect can ruin personal and professional reputations,

leading to job loss and social ostracization. Even after being cleared of the accusations, the stigma of abuse can endure, negatively affecting the target parent's career and personal relationships (Bernet, 2020).

- **<u>Judicial Bias and Prolonged Legal Struggles</u>** – Courts often prioritize caution over fairness, leading to lengthy legal battles for the falsely accused parent. The accused are unfairly burdened with proving their innocence, leading them into costly and emotionally draining legal battles (Warshak, 2015).
- **<u>Use of False Allegations to Justify Alienation</u>** – APs may fabricate neglect or abuse claims as a means to justify cutting off the TP. Some alienating parents invent false medical or psychological conditions for the child, bolstering the claim that the targeted parent is incapable of providing proper care (Harman et al., 2018).
- **<u>Difficulties in Restoring Parent-Child Bond</u>** – Even after disproving false allegations, the damage to the parent-child relationship is often severe and long-lasting. Once a child has been taught to fear or reject the targeted parent, mending the relationship often requires significant intervention, and in many instances, the harm may be permanent (Baker & Verrocchio, 2015).

- **Emotional and Psychological Consequences**
  - TPs often suffer from severe grief, depression, and anxiety due to the loss of their relationship with their child (Harman et al., 2018).
  - Many TPs experience feelings of helplessness and isolation as the legal system often fails to recognize or intervene effectively (Balmer et al., 2018).

- o The rejection leads to parental identity erosion, where TPs struggle to define their role as a parent due to continued alienation (Balmer et al., 2018).
- **Financial and Legal Struggles**
  - o TPs are frequently entangled in ongoing legal battles, as APs use litigation as a tool of control (Lorandos et al., 2013).
  - o High legal costs and repeated court cases can lead to financial ruin, preventing the TP from continuing to fight for their parental rights (Harman et al., 2018).
  - o APs often make false allegations of abuse to justify restricting or terminating the TP's access to the child (Harman & Biringen, 2016).
- **Attempts to Repair the Relationship**
  - o Some TPs try to reconnect with their child through indirect means, such as sending letters or gifts, but these efforts are often intercepted or ridiculed by the AP (Warshak, 2010).
  - o If the child is allowed contact, they may behave coldly, disrespectfully, or ambivalently toward the TP, creating further emotional distress (Verrocchio et al., 2016).
  - o In severe cases, TPs may be forced to disengage completely to protect their own mental health, leading to long-term separation (Warshak, 2015).

Long-Term Impact on the Target Parent

- o Chronic stress, anxiety, and depression (Harman et al., 2018).
- o Social isolation and loss of extended family relationships (Baker & Darnall, 2006).
- o Possible development of PTSD-like symptoms due to prolonged psychological distress (Lorandos et al., 2013).

- **Suicide**
  - According to a 2019 study by Colorado State University, nearly half (47%) of parents experiencing moderate to severe alienation reported having suicidal thoughts within the previous year (Colorado State University, 2019).
  - Research by Lee-Maturana et al. (2020) revealed that 23% of targeted parents had attempted suicide (Lee-Maturana et al., 2020).

Chapter #3: Definitions

14

Chapter #3: Definitions

Alienating Behaviors (AB) / Tactics

Alienating behaviors (AB) refer to a cluster of persistent, coercive, and manipulative actions employed by an alienating parent (AP) with the intent of damaging, undermining, or completely severing the child's relationship with the target parent (TP). These behaviors are not isolated incidents but occur over time, reinforcing a child's negative perception of the TP and potentially leading to complete rejection (Harman et al., 2019). ABs are recognized as a form of psychological abuse and family violence, causing significant emotional distress and long-term harm to the child (Harman et al., 2018).

Key Characteristics of Alienating Behaviors

- **Intentional Psychological Manipulation** – The AP deliberately employs tactics to weaken or destroy the child's bond with the TP (Harman et al., 2019).

- **Repetition Over Time** – ABs are not one-time occurrences; they are used systematically and consistently to alter the child's perception of the TP (Harman et al., 2019).

- **Long-Term Negative Consequences** – Exposure to ABs can lead to emotional, psychological, and social harm, affecting a child's ability to form healthy relationships in adulthood (Harman et al., 2019).

- **Occurs in Both Intact and Non-Intact Families** – While commonly associated with high-conflict divorces, ABs can also be present in intact families where one parent seeks to exert control (Harman et al., 2018).

- **Considered a Form of Family Violence** – ABs function as a form of coercive control, generating fear in the child and exerting power over both the child and the TP (Harman et al., 2019).

- **Instrumental Forms of Aggression** – APs use these behaviors to achieve specific goals, such as legal custody advantages, financial gain, or emotional retaliation against the TP (Harman et al., 2018).
- **Broad Range of Tactics** – Dr. Amy J. Baker has identified 17 specific alienating tactics, but research suggests the number of ABs used is "infinite" and can vary depending on the alienator's motivations and circumstances (Lorandos et al., 2013, p.76).

Flying Monkeys

In the context of parental alienation, a **"flying monkey"** refers to individuals who are manipulated or recruited by an alienating parent to assist in the psychological abuse and denigration of the targeted parent. These individuals—who may include family members, friends, legal professionals, or even therapists—act as proxies, spreading false narratives, reinforcing the alienator's claims, and pressuring the child to reject the other parent. The term originates from the narcissistic abuse framework, where enablers of an abuser (often unwittingly) participate in gaslighting, coercion, and emotional manipulation (Harman et al., 2018; Baker & Eichler, 2016).

Defining Roles:
The Evaluator, The Guardian ad Litem (GAL) & The Mental Health Professional

"The attitude and behavior of professionals accompanying the divorce process ... play an important role in the course of the alienation process."
(Boch-Galhau, 2018)

Key Professionals In Parental Alienation:

#1. Evaluators provide unbiased, evidence-based reports that objectively describe family dynamics and the impact of alienating behaviors on the child, without directly engaging in treatment or advocacy.

#2. Guardian ad Litems (GALs) act as child advocates in court, ensuring that the child's voice and best interests are represented during custody proceedings.

#3. Mental Health Professionals (MHPs) focus on treating emotional distress and individual psychological symptoms through therapy.

Chapter #4: Defining Roles

#1. The Evaluator's Role Parental Alienation

Evaluators provide an objective assessment of parental alienation's impact on a child's well-being. Unlike mental health professionals who offer therapy or GALs who advocate in court, **evaluators remain neutral**, conducting assessments, interviews, and psychological testing. They identify signs of manipulation and alienation, offering the court crucial insights to guide custody decisions and interventions that support the child's emotional stability and parental relationships. Their recommendations can restore the child's sense of security, promoting a balanced relationship with both parents, and preventing further psychological harm.

A. Objective Assessment of Family Dynamics

- Evaluators perform comprehensive assessments of family relationships, conflicts, and patterns of alienating behavior by gathering data from interviews, observations, and collateral sources.
- They identify parental alienation by distinguishing manipulative tactics from genuine concerns for a child's welfare.
- Evaluators must be able to distinguish between real family conflicts and the covert, manipulative behaviors that are characteristic of parental alienation (Bernet, 2020).
- Unlike therapists and GALs, evaluators provide an objective assessment that guides custody determinations and protects the child's long-term welfare (Harman et al., 2018).

B. Best Practices for Helping a Child Experiencing PA

- **Thorough Documentation**: Meticulously collect data on alienating behaviors through interviews, school records, and reports from third parties.
- **Objective Reporting**: Present clear, unbiased findings that distinguish normal parent-child conflict from the harmful effects of alienation.
- **Collaboration**: Work collaboratively with mental health professionals and GALs to ensure that the child's emotional needs are addressed and that the court receives a comprehensive picture of family dynamics.
- **Focus on the Child's Best Interests**: Provide custody recommendations that promote a stable and nurturing environment, facilitating a healthy relationship with both parents.
- Evaluators offer the courts essential, unbiased perspectives that are crucial for safeguarding a child's future well-being in high-conflict custody disputes (Warshak, 2015).

#2. How a Guardian ad Litem (GAL) Can Help a Child Experiencing Parental Alienation

A Guardian ad Litem (GAL) is vital in recognizing and addressing the impact of parental alienation (PA) by advocating for the child's best interests and promoting a healthy bond with both parents. **Their role includes identifying alienating behaviors, ensuring the child receives appropriate psychological support, and making well-informed custody recommendations.** By intervening early and prioritizing the child's emotional well-being, a GAL helps protect against the long-term effects of alienation and fosters the restoration of parent-child relationships.

A. Identifying Signs of Parental Alienation:

- Conduct in-depth interviews with the child, both parents, extended family, teachers, and therapists.
- Evaluate how the child engages with both parents to detect any indicators of undue influence or coercion leading to the rejection of one parent (Harman et al., 2018).
- Identify behaviors like unwarranted fear or hostility toward one parent, which are key indicators of psychological manipulation (Baker, 2010).

B. Ensuring the Child's Emotional Well-being:

- Advocate for court-ordered therapy or reunification counseling to repair damaged parent-child relationships.
- Recommend mental health evaluations if the child exhibits signs of emotional distress, anxiety, or depression.
- **Secures timely psychological support to prevent the effects of alienation from becoming long-lasting or irreversible** (Bernet, 2020).

C. Making Recommendations to the Court:

- Provide a neutral, evidence-based assessment of the child's relationship with both parents.
- Courts depend on GALs to offer an impartial assessment of whether a child's refusal to accept a parent is genuine or caused by inappropriate influence (Harman & Lorandos, 2021).
- Suggest modifications in custody or visitation to prevent further alienation.

D. Monitoring Compliance with Court Orders:

- Ensure that the alienating parent complies with court-mandated therapy, co-parenting counseling, or reunification plans.
- Report violations where one parent continues to engage in alienating tactics.
- In instances of significant alienation, a GAL might suggest temporarily transferring custody to the targeted parent to safeguard the child's emotional and psychological well-being (Baker & Eichler, 2016).
- Use free resources like **TalkingParents.com** to monitor communication between both parents.

E. Advocating for Reunification Efforts:

- Suggest supervised visitation or therapeutic sessions to gradually rebuild the bond with the rejected parent.
- Collaborate with family law experts to design structured interventions that focus on the child's long-term well-being, putting it ahead of short-term parental disputes (Warshak, 2015).

#3. How a Mental Health Professional (MHP) Can Help a Child Experiencing Parental Alienation

Parental alienation severely disrupts a child's sense of security and emotional stability, leading to alienation from the targeted parent. The alienating parent manipulates the child's emotions, creating a distorted perception that fosters rejection, fear, and hostility toward the other parent. MHPs play a crucial role in helping the child rebuild trust, correct emotional estrangement and restore a secure parent-child bond.

A. Assessment and Identification

A mental health professional plays a critical role in identifying and assessing the effects of parental alienation on a child.

This includes:

- **Conducting Clinical Interviews:** Evaluating the child's perception of each parent and identifying signs of manipulation.
- **Using Standardized Tools:** Using The Five-Factor Model of Alienation (Morrison & Ring, 2023)
- **Identifying Alienating Behaviors:** Using the 17 Alienating Behaviors List (Baker, 2020)
- **Recognizing Symptoms:** Using The 8 Behavioral Manifestations of Parental Alienation (Gardner, 1998)

B. Educating and Empowering the Child

A therapist can help the child understand their emotions and experiences:

- **Providing Psychoeducation:** Teaching the child about healthy relationships and the harmful effects of manipulation (Baker & Darnall, 2006).

- **Encouraging Critical Thinking:** Assist children in identifying contradictions within the alienating parent's stories.
- **Cognitive Reframing:** Through therapy, children learn to recognize manipulative tactics and develop a more balanced and independent perspective on both parents.
- **Building Coping Strategies:** Use emotional regulation techniques, such as mindfulness and journaling.
- **Rebuilding Emotional Security:** Therapists provide a safe and neutral space for the child to express their thoughts and feelings, helping them separate their own emotions from external influences.

C. Facilitating Reunification with the Alienated Parent

Therapists can play a role in repairing the child-parent bond:

- **Supervised or Therapeutic Visitation:** Provide a safe, neutral space for interaction.
- **Gradual Exposure Therapy:** Helping the child feel comfortable re-engaging with the alienated parent.
- **Attachment-Based Interventions:** These strategies focus on rebuilding the emotional connection with the targeted parent by addressing fear, mistrust, and false narratives instilled by the alienating parent.

D. Involvement in Legal Proceedings

Mental health professionals may assist in court cases to advocate for the child's best interests:

- **Providing Expert Testimony:** Clarifying the psychological impact of alienation on the child.
- **Recommending Custody Interventions:** Consider using protective measures to ensure the child's long-term wellbeing.
- **Collaborating with Legal Professionals:** To develop parenting plans that minimize continued alienation.

Parental Alienation
is
Psychological Maltreatment

"The psychological foundation of parental alienation—lack of empathy and the inability to tolerate the child's separate needs and perceptions—is also the foundation of psychological maltreatment
(as cited in Baker and Ben Ami 2011, p.473)**"**
(Baker & Verrocchio, 2015)

"Psychological" refers to anything related to the mind, emotions, or mental processes. It encompasses thoughts, feelings, behaviors, and cognitive functions, as well as how individuals perceive and respond to their environment (Chadwick et al., 2014, p.237).

"Maltreatment" refers to the harmful treatment of a person or entity through either actions (commission) or failures to act (omission) (Chadwick et al., 2014, p.237). It is the broadest term, encompassing both abuse, which involves intentional harmful acts, and neglect, which results from a lack of necessary care. Essentially, maltreatment serves as an inclusive term that covers both abusive actions and neglectful inactions (Chadwick et al., 2014, p.237).

According to Baker & Verrocchio (2015) in *Parental Bonding and Parental Alienation as Correlates of Psychological Maltreatment in Adults in Intact and Non-intact Families,* parental alienation (PA) is a profound form of psychological abuse where one parent consistently influences their child to unjustly reject the other parent. This manipulation involves coercive tactics and emotional control, leading the child to harbor unwarranted fear and hostility toward the targeted parent. Consequently, the child may internalize false perceptions, viewing the alienated parent as unsafe or unworthy of affection.

Also, both PA and psychological maltreatment share core elements, notably the repetitive use of manipulative behaviors that harm a child's emotional health. Such actions disrupt the child's essential needs for love, security, and stability, fostering negative emotions like fear and guilt toward the alienated parent. In parental alienation, these coercive strategies distort the child's understanding, leading to the acceptance of false narratives that eventually damage the parent-child relationship.

Similar to coercive control observed in family violence, PA creates an unhealthy emotional dependency on the alienating parent. This dynamic employs fear and loyalty manipulation to erode the child's connection with the targeted parent. The enduring effects of PA are comparable to those seen in psychological maltreatment, heightening the risk of anxiety, depression, and emotional distress. Additionally, PA can adversely affect a child's self-esteem, trust in relationships, and overall psychological development.

Psychological maltreatment encompasses 6 various subtypes, including:

- **Spurning** – Verbal and nonverbal behaviors that reject, belittle, or degrade the child (APSAC, 2019).
- **Terrorizing** – Creating an environment of fear through threats, intimidation, or coercion (APSAC, 2019).
- **Isolating** – Restricting the child's social interactions, preventing healthy relationships (APSAC, 2019).
- **Exploiting/Corrupting** – Encouraging maladaptive behaviors such as deception, criminal activity, or inappropriate caregiving roles (APSAC, 2019).

- **Denying Emotional Responsiveness** – Failing to provide warmth, affection, or support (APSAC, 2019).
- **Neglecting Medical, Mental Health, or Educational Needs** – Willfully disregarding the child's essential care and development (Baker et al., 2021).

Chapter #5: PA Is PM

The 6 Subtypes of Psychological Maltreatment & How They Connect to Parental Alienation

"The American Professional Society on the Abuse of Children (APSAC) are consistent with other definitional systems & can be used to reliably code child protection records, are based on research that documents the damage caused by this form of maltreatment, are cross-culturally valid & are consistent with definitions used by governments & other professional organizations."

(American Professional Society on the Abuse of Children [APSAC], 2019)

#1. **Spurning** (Rejecting, Degrading, or Humiliating the Child)
Encompasses both verbal and nonverbal actions by a caregiver that reject or demean a child (APSAC, 2019).

As outlined in Harman et al. (2018), *Parental Alienating Behaviors: An Unacknowledged Form of Family Violence:*

Spurning is a form of psychological maltreatment in which a caregiver rejects or devalues a child, causing the child to feel unloved, unworthy, or inherently defective (Baker et al., 2021; Hart et al., 2017). This behavior may involve constant criticism, verbal insults, ridicule, humiliation, or ignoring the child's emotional needs (Glaser, 2011). In the context of parental alienation, the alienating parent might spurn the child for showing affection toward the targeted parent, deepening the child's sense of guilt and emotional conflict.

These behaviors not only damage the child's self-esteem and emotional well-being but also create a deep sense of insecurity and rejection. In the context of parental alienation, spurning is often used to reinforce the belief that the targeted parent does not love or care for the child, further cementing the child's rejection of that parent and increasing their emotional dependency on the alienating parent.

Belittling and Degrading: An alienating parent might frequently tell the child they are "stupid" or "worthless," especially when they express a desire to see the targeted parent. For example, if a child says, "I miss Dad," the alienating parent might respond, *"Why would you miss someone who abandoned you?"*

- **Shaming and Ridiculing Normal Emotions:** If the child expresses sadness about missing the targeted parent, the alienating parent may mock them, saying, *"Oh, are you going to cry now? You're just like your weak, pathetic mother."*

- **Singling Out One Child for Criticism or Punishment:** An alienating parent may target one child, blaming them for family problems, while favoring a sibling who aligns with their views. For instance, they might say, *"Your brother is smart enough to see how awful your dad is—why aren't you?"* They may also force the child to do extra chores as a form of punishment for wanting a relationship with the targeted parent.

- **Public Humiliation:** The alienating parent might make derogatory comments about the child in front of others, such as saying at a school event, *"This one is just like his deadbeat father—good-for-nothing and unreliable."* They may also post on social media about how "disrespectful" or "ungrateful" the child is for wanting to see the targeted parent.

- **Using Humiliation To Mock TP:** The alienating parent (AP) may use humiliation as a way to demean and discredit the targeted parent (TP). This can involve making fun of the TP's interests, personality traits, career, or relationships with friends and family (as cited in Baker & Darnall, 2006; Harman & Biringen, 2018). The AP may also draw attention to the TP's flaws or past mistakes to shape a negative perception in the child's mind (as cited in Warshak, 2015c). For instance, one TP shared with an author that the AP would place him on speakerphone during calls with their children and ridicule him throughout the conversation, aiming to make the children view him as laughable or insignificant.

Examples of What A Child Might Say to a Counselor:

- *"My mom/dad says my other parent is selfish and never really wanted me."*
- *"I was told that if I loved my other parent, it means I don't love my mom/dad."*
- *"My mom/dad says my other parent has never done anything for me and that I owe them nothing."*
- *"My mom/dad laughs and calls my other parent a loser every time I mention their name."*
- *"I was told that my other parent only pretends to love me to look good in court."*

Chapter #6: 6 Subtypes of PM

Chapter #6: 6 Subtypes of PM

#2. <u>Exploiting</u>/<u>Corrupting</u>

(Manipulating the child to support the alienation)

Encompasses caregiver actions that promote or reinforce harmful behaviors in the child, such as encouraging self-destructive tendencies, antisocial conduct, criminal activity, deviance, or other maladaptive patterns of behavior (APSAC, 2019).

As outlined in Harman et al. (2018), *Parental Alienating Behaviors: An Unacknowledged Form of Family Violence:*

Exploiting and corrupting behaviors involve manipulating a child into adopting inappropriate beliefs, attitudes, or actions that serve the needs of the alienating parent at the expense of the child's well-being (Baker et al., 2021; Hart et al., 2017). In cases of parental alienation, alienating parents may expose children to adult conflicts, legal disputes, or financial burdens, forcing them to take sides and assume responsibilities beyond their developmental capacity.

Children may also be coerced into spying on or sabotaging the targeted parent, lying in court proceedings, or engaging in other deceptive behaviors that compromise their moral development and emotional stability (Baker & Verrocchio, 2015; Warshak, 2015). By distorting the child's sense of right and wrong, alienating parents reinforce dependency, obstruct the child's autonomy, and further deepen the psychological divide between the child and the targeted parent (Harman & Biringen, 2016).

- **Encouraging Antisocial Behavior:** An alienating parent may introduce the child to substance abuse, involve them in criminal activities, or pressure them into deceptive actions, reinforcing deviant behavior. For example, a parent might allow a child to steal from the other parent and justify it as "payback."

- **Promoting Developmentally Inappropriate Roles:** The alienating parent may assign the child adult responsibilities, such as acting as a caretaker or confidant, known as parentification. For instance, they might tell the child, "You're the only one who understands me," forcing them into an emotional support role beyond their years.

- **Suppressing Autonomy:** The parent may discourage independence by micromanaging the child's life, dictating their opinions, and rejecting any expressions of individuality. For example, if the child expresses love for the targeted parent, the alienating parent might say, *"You're not allowed to talk like that in this house."*
- **Interfering with Cognitive Development:** An alienating parent may distort reality by manipulating the child's perception of events, restricting access to differing viewpoints, or discouraging critical thinking. For example, they might insist, *"Everything your other parent says is a lie,"* preventing the child from forming their own judgments.

Examples of What A Child Might Say to a Counselor:

- *"I have to spy on my mom/dad and tell my other parent everything they do."*
- *"I'm supposed to tell the judge that I don't want to see my other parent, even though I do."*
- *"My mom/dad told me to lie and say I was scared of my other parent in court."*
- *"I was told to record my mom/dad without them knowing so we could catch them doing something bad."*
- *"I'm supposed to agree with everything my mom/dad says about my other parent, or they get really mad.*

#3. <u>Terrorizing</u> (Instilling Fear or Forcing Loyalty to the Alienator)
Involves caregiver actions that intimidate, endanger, or cause the child to fear physical harm, abandonment, death, or the loss of loved ones or valued possessions by placing them in clearly threatening or hazardous situations (APSAC, 2019).

As outlined in Harman et al. (2018), *Parental Alienating Behaviors: An Unacknowledged Form of Family Violence:*

Terrorizing is a form of psychological maltreatment in which a caregiver deliberately induces fear, anxiety, or intense emotional distress in a child through threats, coercion, or by exposing them to harmful or frightening situations (Baker et al., 2021; Hart et al., 2017). This may involve threatening the child, yelling aggressively, sudden angry outbursts, or making the child witness or participate in the humiliation of another person (Glaser, 2011). In the context of parental alienation, the alienating parent may use terrorizing tactics by convincing the child that the targeted parent is unsafe, abusive, or deceitful—creating fear and unease around spending time with that parent.

These behaviors not only create a deep sense of insecurity, anxiety, and helplessness in the child but also reinforce the alienating parent's control. By instilling irrational fear toward the targeted parent, the alienating parent ensures the child's loyalty, making reunification with the targeted parent increasingly difficult (Baker & Darnall, 2006; Warshak, 2015).

- **Unpredictable or Chaotic Environment:** An alienating parent may frequently change rules, schedules, or living arrangements without warning, leaving the child feeling anxious and insecure. For example, *"Pack your things! You're going to live with your other parent now because I'm done with you!"*—only to later reverse the decision.
- **Exposing the Child to Dangerous Situations:** The parent may leave the child alone in unsafe environments or expose them to harmful individuals. For instance, they may refuse to pick up the child from an unsafe location out of spite toward the other parent.

- **Unrealistic Expectations with Threats:** The alienating parent may set impossible standards, saying, *"If you don't completely reject your other parent, I'll take away everything you love."* The child may be punished for showing affection toward the targeted parent.
- **Threats or Acts of Violence Against the Child:** They might scream, *"If you mention your other parent again, I'll make you sorry!"* or physically intimidate the child by slamming doors, throwing objects, or grabbing them forcefully.
- **Threats or Violence Toward Loved Ones or Objects**: The alienating parent may say, *"If you keep seeing your other parent, I'll get rid of your favorite toy,"* or destroy photos, gifts, or belongings associated with the targeted parent to reinforce fear and compliance.

Examples of What A Child Might Say to a Counselor:

- *"I get in trouble if I say anything nice about my other parent."*
- *"My mom/dad told me that if I go to my other parent's house, I might never see them again."*
- *"I was told that my other parent would try to kidnap me if I spent time with him/her."*
- *"My mom/dad said if I see my other parent, I will ruin their life."*
- *"My mom/dad told me that my other parent is dangerous, but I don't understand why."*

#4. Denying Emotional Responsiveness

(Withholding Love or Affection if the Child Shows Attachment to the TP)
Includes caregiver acts that ignore the child's attempts & needs to interact (eg, failing to express affection, caring & love for the child) & showing no emotion in interactions with the child (APSAC, 2019).

As outlined in Harman et al. (2018), *Parental Alienating Behaviors: An Unacknowledged Form of Family Violence:*

Withholding emotional responsiveness is a type of psychological maltreatment in which a caregiver consistently fails to acknowledge, respond to, or support a child's emotional needs (Baker et al., 2021; Hart et al., 2017). This can include ignoring a child's distress, refusing to offer comfort, or withholding affection and validation (Glaser, 2011). In the context of parental alienation, the alienating parent may intentionally withdraw love or approval when the child shows affection for the targeted parent, effectively teaching the child to suppress their emotions in order to avoid rejection or disapproval (Baker & Verrocchio, 2015; Harman et al., 2018).

These behaviors not only erode the child's sense of self-worth and emotional security but also further the alienation by making the targeted parent appear unnecessary or unworthy of love. Over time, the child may internalize the belief that expressing emotions—especially love for the targeted parent—is unacceptable, leading to emotional detachment and long-term relational difficulties (Baker & Darnall, 2006; Warshak, 2015).

- **Ignoring the Child's Attempts for Connection:**
  - Refusing to acknowledge when the child seeks comfort, affection, or validation (*e.g., when the child expresses missing the targeted parent, the alienating parent dismisses or punishes them*).
  - Avoiding physical touch, eye contact, or emotional engagement (*e.g., ignoring the child's attempts to hug or speak about their feelings*).

- **Withholding Affection and Love:**
  - *Failing to express warmth, care, or encouragement (e.g., never saying "I love you" or offering praise, especially when the child mentions the targeted parent).*
  - *Using love and approval as a conditional tool (e.g., showing affection only when the child rejects the targeted parent).*
- **Emotional Detachment:**
  - Interacting with the child in a cold, distant manner, showing little to no response to their emotions (*e.g., remaining expressionless when the child expresses sadness about missing the targeted parent*).
  - Refusing to participate in emotional bonding activities (*e.g., not celebrating achievements unless they align with the alienating parent's expectations*).
- **Dismissing Emotional Needs:**
  - Ignoring when the child is upset, lonely, or scared and refusing to provide reassurance (*e.g., invalidating the child's feelings by saying, "You shouldn't feel that way about them"*).
  - Ridiculing or shaming the child for expressing love or longing for the targeted parent (*e.g., rolling their eyes, scoffing, or saying, "Why would you miss someone who abandoned you?"*).

Examples of What A Child Might Say to Counselor:

- *"When I came back from my visit, my mom/dad wouldn't talk to me for hours."*
- *"If I say I miss my other parent, my mom/dad ignores me and walks away."*
- *"I get the silent treatment if I don't agree with what my mom/dad says about my other parent."*
- *"If I visit my other parent, I'm not allowed to hug my mom/dad when I get home."*
- *"My mom/dad only pays attention to me when I say I don't like my other parent."*

#5. <u>Isolating</u>

(Restricting the Child's Access to the Targeted Parent or Support Systems)
Includes ongoing behavior by a caregiver that systematically limits the child's ability to interact or communicate with others—whether peers or adults—both at home and in external settings (APSAC, 2019). **Such restrictions can hinder the child's social development and emotional well-being.**

As outlined in Harman et al. (2018), *Parental Alienating Behaviors: An Unacknowledged Form of Family Violence:*

Isolating is a form of psychological maltreatment in which a caregiver deliberately restricts a child's social interactions and relationships, cutting them off from sources of support, affection, and normal developmental experiences (Hart et al., 2017). In cases of parental alienation, isolating is used as a tactic to sever the child's bond with the targeted parent by limiting communication, preventing visits, and discouraging or outright forbidding interactions with the targeted parent's extended family and friends (Baker & Darnall, 2006; Harman et al., 2018).

Alienating parents may enforce strict boundaries that make the child feel disloyal or guilty for wanting to see the targeted parent, further deepening their dependency on the alienating parent (Verrocchio et al., 2016). The child may be told that the targeted parent is dangerous, unloving, or uninterested in them, reinforcing their emotional and physical separation (Baker & Verrocchio, 2015).

These behaviors not only deprive the child of meaningful relationships and emotional security but also increase their susceptibility to manipulation by the alienating parent. Over time, the lack of exposure to the targeted parent results in the child adopting the alienating parent's distorted narratives, leading to a complete rejection of the targeted parent and an impaired ability to form healthy relationships in adulthood (Baker et al., 2021; Warshak, 2015).

- **Isolating the Child from Supportive Relationships:**
  - Preventing the child from seeing or speaking with the targeted parent (*e.g., blocking phone calls, intercepting messages, or making excuses to cancel visits*).
  - Prohibiting the child from spending time with extended family members who support the targeted parent (*e.g., forbidding visits with grandparents, aunts, or uncles who maintain a relationship with the alienated parent*).
- **Restricting Social Interaction with Peers:**
  - Controlling or limiting friendships (*e.g., not allowing the child to attend social events if they have expressed a desire to see the targeted parent*).
  - Enforcing extreme rules that isolate the child (*e.g., "You can only have friends who agree with us about your other parent"*).
- **Blocking Outside Support Systems:**
  - Discouraging or forbidding the child from speaking to teachers, counselors, or mentors about their feelings (*e.g., warning the child, "Don't tell anyone about what happens at home, or they'll take you away"*).
  - Interfering with therapy or counseling that might help the child reconnect with the targeted parent (*e.g., refusing to allow court-ordered reunification therapy*).
- **Monitoring and Controlling Communication:**
  - Reading or deleting messages between the child and the targeted parent (*e.g., taking the child's phone and removing voicemails or texts*).
  - Forcing the child to block or "unfriend" the targeted parent on social media (*e.g., making the child remove pictures or posts that include the alienated parent*).

Chapter #6: 6 Subtypes of PM

Examples of What A Child Might Say to Counselor:

- *"My mom/dad won't let me call or text my other parent."*
- *"I'm not allowed to talk to my grandparents because they still talk to my other mom/dad."*
- *"My mom/dad said I have to block my other parent on social media.*
- *"If I bring up my other mom/dad, my other parent tells me to stop talking about them."*
- *"I had to throw away pictures of my other parent because it made my mom/dad upset."*

Chapter #6: 6 Subtypes of PM

#6. Mental Health, Medical & Educational Neglect

(Using Alienation to Sabotage the Child's Well-being)

Includes unwarranted caregiver acts that ignore, refuse to allow, or fail to provide the necessary treatment for the mental health, medical and educational problems or needs for the child (APSAC, 2019).

As outlined in Harman et al. (2018), *Parental Alienating Behaviors: An Unacknowledged Form of Family Violence:*

Mental health, medical, and educational neglect occur when a caregiver fails to meet a child's basic needs in these critical areas, either by withholding necessary care, providing excessive or inappropriate treatment, or obstructing access to essential services (Baker et al., 2021; Hart et al., 2017). In the context of parental alienation, alienating parents may neglect or manipulate medical, psychological, and educational needs as a means of maintaining control over the child and furthering the rejection of the targeted parent.

For example, an alienating parent might deny a child needed medical care, exaggerate or fabricate illnesses to limit the targeted parent's involvement, or deliberately obstruct the child's access to mental health professionals who could identify signs of alienation (Warshak, 2010). Educational neglect is also common, with alienating parents allowing excessive absences, interfering with academic success, or using school as a means to limit the targeted parent's parenting time (Harman & Biringen, 2016).

These behaviors not only jeopardize the child's well-being and future success but also serve to deepen their dependence on the alienating parent, reinforcing the alienation process (Baker & Verrocchio, 2015; Warshak, 2015).

- **Examples of Mental Health Neglect:**
  - **Minimizing Emotional Distress:** Dismissing or trivializing the child's emotional struggles, such as labeling their sadness about missing the targeted parent as "overreacting" or "being dramatic.

- ○ **Obstructing Access to Mental Health Support:** Actively preventing the child from receiving counseling, including canceling appointments, undermining the credibility of the therapist, or insisting therapy is unnecessary.
- **Examples of Medical Neglect:**
  - ○ **Neglecting Medical Needs:** Ignoring or refusing essential medical care, such as doctor visits, prescribed medications, or recommended treatments (e.g., claiming "they just need to toughen up").
  - ○ **Manipulating Through Illness:** Fabricating or exaggerating health concerns to interfere with the child's time with the targeted parent, such as falsely claiming the child is "too ill" to attend visitation.
- **Examples of Educational Neglect:**
  - ○ **Interfering with Academic Progress:** Disrupting the child's education by preventing school attendance, discouraging homework completion, or withholding participation in school activities if the child expresses interest in the targeted parent or if the child might see the TP at a school function.
  - ○ **Limiting Future Opportunities:** Discouraging or blocking the child from pursuing academic or career paths that promote independence or bring them closer to the targeted parent—such as applying to colleges near that parent.

Examples of What A Child Might Say to Counselor:

- "My mom/dad won't let me see a therapist because they think the therapist will make me want to see my other parent."
- "My mom/dad refuses to take me to the doctor because my other parent would find out."
- "I missed school because my mom/dad didn't want my other parent to pick me up."

- *"I wasn't allowed to do my homework because my mom/dad said school doesn't matter."*
- *"My mom/dad won't let me take my medication because they think my other parent is overreacting."*

Chapter #6: 6 Subtypes of PM

Chapter #6: 6 Subtypes of PM

Is It Parental Alienation?
The Five-Factor Model (FFM)

**"...the Five-Factor Model as an assessment tool for the occurrence of PA
<u>has been determined to be valid and reliable.</u>"**

(Morrison & Ring, 2023, p.16)

<u>These 5 Factors Must Be Present for PA to Exist:</u>

1. The child exhibits refusal to engage in contact with a parent.
2. The child previously shared a positive relationship with the now-rejected parent.
3. The absence of any abuse, neglect, or seriously deficient parenting by the rejected parent.
4. The alienating parent engages in various behaviors identified among the 17 primary parental alienation strategies like those outlined by Dr. Amy J.L. Baker. (17)
5. The child exhibits attitudes that align with the 8 specific behavioral irregularities identified by Dr. Richard Gardner (8)

(Morrison & Ring, 2023, p.16)

Chapter #7: Is It PA? The Five Factor Model

How to Apply the Five-Factor Model from an Evaluator's Perspective

When assessing parental alienation using the Five-Factor Model, evaluators must carefully analyze each factor based on objective evidence, clinical observations, and corroborated information. Below is a guide for evaluators to systematically approach each factor:

Factor 1: The Child Resists or Refuses Contact with One Parent

- Observe the child's behavior toward the rejected parent.
- Determine whether the resistance is consistent and persistent.
- Gather information from multiple sources, including interviews, school reports, and third-party observations.
- Consider whether the child's rejection is situational or generalized across all interactions.

  (Morrison & Ring, 2023, p.16)

Factor 2: A Prior Positive Relationship with the Rejected Parent

- Review historical records, photographs, and testimonials that document the parent-child relationship before alienation occurred.
- Interview both parents, extended family, and other relevant individuals who witnessed the prior bond.
- Assess the quality of past interactions and whether the rejected parent previously played an active and nurturing role.

  (Morrison & Ring, 2023, p.16)

Factor 3: No History of Abuse, Neglect, or Severely Deficient Parenting by the Rejected Parent

- Conduct a thorough review of allegations, including legal records, child protective service reports, and prior custody evaluations.
- Verify if any accusations of abuse or neglect are substantiated with credible evidence.
- Distinguish between legitimate concerns and unsubstantiated claims that may be influenced by parental conflict.
(Morrison & Ring, 2023, p.16)

Factor 4: The Favored Parent Engages in Alienating Behaviors

- Identify patterns of alienating tactics, such as badmouthing, restricting communication, or interfering with visitation.
- Examine written correspondence, court filings, and recorded statements that may indicate manipulation.
- Consider expert literature on alienating behaviors to determine whether the favored parent's actions align with known parental alienation tactics.
(Morrison & Ring, 2023, p.16)

Factor 5: The Child Displays Multiple Behavioral Signs of Alienation

Assess the presence of the eight behavioral irregularities of alienation identified by Dr. Richard Gardner (e.g., lack of ambivalence, independent thinker phenomenon, reflexive support for the favored parent).

(*see Criteria for Diagnosis Of PA 8 Behaviors)

- Evaluate whether the child's reasoning for rejecting the parent is disproportionate or lacks a rational basis.

- Look for inconsistencies in the child's statements that may suggest external influence.
(Morrison & Ring, 2023, p.16)

Conclusion

Evaluators must base their assessments on objective data, avoiding assumptions or biases. A comprehensive analysis of all five factors allows for a well-rounded determination of whether parental alienation is occurring. Proper documentation and professional judgment are critical to ensuring an accurate and fair evaluation. (Morrison & Ring, 2023, p.16)

Chapter #7: Is It PA? The Five Factor Model

54
Chapter #7: Is It PA? The Five Factor Model

The 17 Primary PA Strategies
(by Dr. Amy J.L.Baker)

"There are seventeen primary parental alienation strategies that have been identified through research studies with adults who were alienated as children and with targeted parents. These 17 PA strategies have been validated in a series of subsequent studies."

(Amy J.L. Baker, Phd: Parental alienation, 2025)

Research has identified 17 parental alienation strategies, which can be categorized into five overarching themes: isolation, fear, undermining authority, erasing & false memory implantation, and encouraging betrayal. These tactics are used by an alienating parent to manipulate a child's perception of the targeted parent, leading to emotional isolation and psychological harm.

- **Isolation:** The alienating parent limits or completely cuts off the child's contact with the targeted parent, extended family, and friends, creating an environment where the child is solely influenced by the alienator (2025).
- **Fear:** The child is subjected to threats, intimidation, or exaggerated narratives that paint the targeted parent as dangerous or untrustworthy, instilling anxiety and reluctance to maintain a relationship (2025).
- **Undermining Authority:** The alienating parent portrays the targeted parent as incompetent, unloving, or unfit, diminishing their

authority and creating conflict between the child and the alienated parent (2025).

- **Erasing & False Memory Implantation**: The child is manipulated into believing past events occurred differently or are completely fabricated, often through repetitive suggestions, leading to distorted or false memories about the targeted parent (2025).
- **Encouraging Betrayal:** The alienating parent rewards the child for rejecting or spying on the targeted parent, reinforcing disloyalty while framing emotional detachment as a necessary act of self-protection (2025).

The 17 Primary Strategies That Contribute to PA

☐ 1. Criticizing the other parent to the child to create the impression that the other parent is unsafe, unloving, and unavailable.

☐ 2. Restricting the child's interactions with the other parent, hindering their ability to participate meaningfully in each other's lives.

☐ 3. Disrupting the child's communication with the other parent, preventing emotional connection during periods of separation.

☐ 4. Hindering the child's ability to think about, discuss, or view photographs of the other parent, thereby weakening their bond.

☐ 5. Refusing to show affection & love to the child when he/she shows interest in the other parent.

☐ 6. Permitting the child to decide whether to spend time with the other parent, thereby implying that such time is optional and undesirable.

☐ 7. Coercing the child into rejecting the other parent.

☐ 8. Informing the child that the other parent does not love him/her.

☐ 9. Portraying the other parent as dangerous or untrustworthy.

☐ 10. Involving the child in discussions about personal and legal matters to elicit feelings of hurt and anger toward the other parent.

☐ 11. Encouraging the child to be a "secret agent" & gather information about the other parent's personal matters.

☐ 12. Encouraging the child to conceal information from the target parent & to keep it between the alienator and child only.

☐ 13. Addressing the other parent by their first name instead of "Mom" or "Dad."

☐ 14. Addressing a new significant other as "mom" or "dad."

☐ 15. Altering a child's name to eliminate association with the other parent

☐ 16. Concealing information from the other parent.

☐ 17. Sabotaging the other parent's authority.

(Baker, 2007)

58

Chapter #8: The 17 Primary Alienating Strategies

Criteria for Diagnosis of Parental Alienation
8 Behaviors
(by Dr. Richard Gardner)

"The presence and degree of PA are diagnosed on the basis of the behavior observed in a child, not on the basis of the degree of manipulation to which the child is exposed."

(Boch-Galhau, 2018)

These 2 Core Behaviors Are Required for a Parental Alienation Diagnosis:

#1. A Concerted Effort to Disparage the Target Parent

- The child frequently expresses complaints, often trivial, false, or irrational.
- The child denies ever having positive experiences with the target parent, despite evidence to the contrary.
- Alienated children tend to avoid any opportunities for reconciliation.

(Lorandos et al., 2013, p. 17)

Example Statements:

- *"I've never had a single good moment with my dad. He's always been mean and scary."*
- *"Mom never did anything for me. I don't even think she loves me."*
- *"I hate going to his house—it's the worst place ever!"*

#2. Weak or Trivial Justifications for the Child's Disapproval of the Target Parent

The child's negative reactions, such as hatred or disdain, are extreme and unjustified.

- The child may claim fear of the target parent but does not display typical fear responses.

(Lorandos et al., 2013, p. 17)

Example Statements:

- *"I don't know why, but I just know she's a bad person."*
- *"I'm scared of him, but I can't say why."*
- *"Everything about her is just wrong."*

At Least 2 of the Following 6 Attitudes and Behaviors Must Be Present for PA to Exist:

#1. An Unwavering Negative Stance Against the TP

- The child exhibits black-and-white thinking, idealizing the alienating parent while completely devaluing the target parent.

(Lorandos et al., 2013, p. 17)

Example Statements:

- *"Dad is the best parent in the world, and Mom is just terrible."*
- *"Everything bad in my life is because of my mother."*

#2. Child Insists Negative Feelings Toward the TP Are Entirely His/Her Own

- The child insists that rejecting the target parent is entirely their own decision, denying any influence from the alienating parent.

(Lorandos et al., 2013, p. 17)

Example Statements:

- *"No one told me to hate her—I figured it out myself."*
- *"I just woke up one day and knew I didn't want to see Dad anymore."*

#3. Automatic, Unwavering Allegiance to the AP

- The child automatically takes the alienating parent's side in conflicts, without critical reasoning.

(Lorandos et al., 2013, p. 17)

Example Statements:

- *"Mom says Dad is a liar, so that must be true."*
- *"I don't care what the judge says—Dad is right about everything."*

#4. Lack of Remorse for the Mistreatment of the TP

- The child may act oppositional, rude, disrespectful, or even violent toward the target parent, showing no remorse.

(Lorandos et al., 2013, p. 17)

Example Statements:

- *"I screamed at my mom and called her names, but she deserves it."*
- *"I don't feel bad at all for ignoring my dad's calls—he should leave me alone."*

#5. Child Adopts Narratives or Accusations to Justify Alienation

- The child repeats scripted statements from the alienating parent.
- Younger siblings may echo what older siblings say.

- The child struggles to elaborate on the events they claim to have experienced.

(Lorandos et al., 2013, p. 17)

Example Statements:

- *"He did something really bad, but I can't remember what it was."*
- *"Mom told me she has proof that Dad is dangerous."*

#6. Child's Hostility Extends Beyond TP to Family, Friends, Relatives

- The child's hostility extends to the target parent's relatives and friends, even when little or no contact has occurred.
- Occasionally, hatred extends to the target parent's pets.

(Lorandos et al., 2013, p. 17)

Example Statements:

- *"I don't want to see Grandma because she's just like my dad."*
- *"Even my dad's dog makes me angry."*

Chapter #9: 8 Behaviors: Criteria for the Diagnosis of PA

The 3 Levels of Severity of Parental Alienation

The Extent of a Child's Alienation from the Target Parent Depends On:

1. The specific alienating tactics employed
2. The combination of tactics used together
3. The frequency of occurrence
4. The length of time tactics are in use
5. The severity and intensity of the tactics
6. The child's age and personality traits
7. The amount of meaningful parenting time the target parent has spent with the child
8. The strength of the child's relationship with the targeted parent before the alienation began

(Harman et al., 2018, pp.1275-1299) (Harman et al., 2019, pp.2-3)

Chapter #10: The 3 Levels of Severity of PA

The 3 Levels of Severity of Parental Alienation

Mild Alienation

Alienator / Parent: "Naïve" or "mild" alienators occasionally exhibit one or two alienating behaviors without the deliberate intent to damage or disrupt the child's relationship with the other parent (Bernet et al., 2022).

Child's Response: In cases of mild alienation, the child may initially resist contact with the targeted parent but expresses enjoyment once interaction occurs (Boch-Galhau, 2018).

When dealing with mild alienation, keep these in mind:

As outlined in Lorandos et al., *Parental Alienation: The Handbook for Mental Health and Legal Professionals* (2013, p.81):

1. Recognizing Alienating Behaviors

- The initial step in tackling parental alienation involves recognizing the behaviors that fuel it. These can include speaking negatively about the other parent, limiting or blocking communication, making unfounded allegations, or manipulating the child's view in a damaging manner.

2. Understanding the Impact on Children

- Parents must recognize that alienating behaviors can have lasting psychological and emotional consequences for children. These include anxiety, depression, difficulty forming healthy relationships, and struggles with self-identity.

3. Educating Parents Engaging in Mild Alienation

- Parents who engage in mild alienation often do not require therapy but benefit from education.

- Many are open to change once they understand the damage their behavior causes.
- Education can come from workshops, professional guidance, and credible literature.

4. Providing Access to Reliable Resources

For Free Evidence-Based Resources on Parental Alienation, visit
>>   ParentalAlienationSpeaks.com   <<

Identifying Early Signs of Alienation

Recognizing the early warning signs of parental alienation is essential to preventing it from progressing into a more entrenched and damaging form. As outlined in *Parental Alienation: The Handbook for Mental Health and Legal Professionals* (Lorandos et al., 2013), early stages of alienation—often referred to as mild alienation—are marked by subtle but concerning behaviors.

In these early phases, a child may voice criticism or show reluctance toward spending time with the targeted parent. Yet, once separated from the influence of the alienating parent or given time to settle in, they may still enjoy and engage in meaningful time together. This behavioral shift is a critical indicator that the child's rejection is not yet rigid or absolute. However, in the presence of the alienating parent, the child may appear emotionally distant, overly critical, or unresponsive to affection.

A frequent expression from a mildly alienated child might be, "I don't want to see you this weekend." For the targeted parent, such words can be devastating. These moments often bring a flood of self-doubt: "What did I do wrong?" or "Is my ex turning my child against me?" The child's demeanor may seem abrupt or out of character, intensifying the emotional sting of rejection.

Chapter #10: The 3 Levels of Severity of PA

Despite this, children in the mild stages of alienation are still capable of forming their own views. They haven't yet fully adopted the alienating parent's narrative and can tolerate conflicting perspectives about past experiences. Their capacity for independent thought remains intact, which means intervention and healing are still very much possible.

It's also important to recognize that children naturally experience emotional ups and downs with their parents—feeling angry one moment and seeking comfort the next. **What distinguishes alienation from normal conflict is the child's persistent inability to let go of that anger.** As Lorandos and colleagues emphasize (2013, pp. 75–77), most children resolve their grievances over time. But in alienation, resentment festers and becomes a tool used to justify continued rejection. If a child's anger feels disproportionate or permanent, it's vital to ask: *What's preventing reconciliation?* In many cases, the answer lies in the continued psychological influence of an alienating parent.

Chapter #10: The 3 Levels of Severity of PA

Moderate Alienation

Alienating Parent/Alienator: Moderate or "active" alienators exhibit **multiple** alienating behaviors and are resistant to change or correction (Bernet et al., 2022).

Child's Response: In cases of moderate alienation, the child adamantly refuses contact with the targeted parent but will reconnect once the alienating parent is not present (Boch-Galhau, 2018).

As outlined in Lorandos et al., *Parental Alienation: The Handbook for Mental Health and Legal Professionals* (2013, pp. 80, 99-100):

- **In moderate PA**, all 8 primary manifestations of alienation are typically present, showing more intensity than in mild cases but not reaching the severity of extreme alienation.
- **Moderate PA** is distinctly more entrenched than mild PA but does not reach the severity of extreme alienation, where rejection becomes nearly irreversible.
- **Need for Professional Help:** Moderately alienating parents can benefit from therapy, as they often struggle with feelings of betrayal or unresolved pain from a contentious divorce.
- **Emotional Outbursts:** These parents may have episodes of rage, during which they direct harsh, emotionally charged tirades at their children, often fueled by lingering resentment toward their ex-spouse.
- **Willingness to Seek Help:** Many moderately alienating parents recognize that their behavior is harmful to both themselves and their children. As a result, they may accept professional guidance to regulate their emotions and begin the healing process.
- **Capacity for Remorse:** Unlike severely alienating parents, those in the moderate category are capable of acknowledging the damage they are causing and expressing guilt for their actions.
- **Recognition of the Target Parent's Role:** When in a rational state, they may support the idea that their children benefit from a loving relationship with the targeted parent.

- **Child's Behavior During Transitions:** A child experiencing moderate PA is actively engaged in a campaign of denigration, particularly during custody transitions.
- **Fluctuating Behavior:** The target parent should anticipate mood swings during visits. Initially, the child may act according to the expectations set by the alienating parent—displaying hostility or emotional distance—especially during transitions between households. However, as time passes, the child may begin to relax and enjoy their time with the targeted parent.
- **Manipulation Through Fear:** Phone calls or check-ins from the alienating parent during the child's visit serve as subtle reinforcements, reminding the child to remain wary of the targeted parent.
- **Undermining Acts:** The alienating parent may use tactics such as giving the child money to diminish the perceived value of gifts or experiences provided by the targeted parent.
- **Sibling Recruitment:** Alienated siblings are often enlisted as allies by the alienating parent, pressuring younger children to join in the rejection of the targeted parent.

Severe Alienation

Alienating Parent: Severe or "Obsessed" alienators engage in **persistent, frequent, and numerous** alienating behaviors with **no intent or capacity to change**. Their primary goal is to completely sever the child's relationship with the targeted parent. (Bernet et al., 2022)

Child's Response: In severe alienation, the child completely rejects the targeted parent, firmly believing—without valid reason—that the parent is dangerous, unworthy, or unloving (Boch-Galhau, 2018).

As outlined in Lorandos et al., *Parental Alienation: The Handbook for Mental Health and Legal Professionals* (2013, pp. 126-130):

- **Multidimensional Impact:** Severe alienation affects a child's behavior, emotions, and cognition (as cited in Gardner, 1998; Kelly, 2010).
- **Extreme Rejection:** Unlike mild or moderate cases, severely alienated children completely reject the targeted parent with intense negativity.
- **Polarized Thinking:** The child views one parent as entirely good and the other as completely bad, often rewriting history to erase positive memories of the rejected parent.
- **Total Avoidance:** The child actively refuses contact with the targeted parent, may sever ties with their extended family, and often threatens to defy court-ordered visitation.
- **Hostile Behavior:** Interactions with the rejected parent are characterized by extreme defiance, disobedience, hostility, and emotional withdrawal.
- The child may resist or refuse contact, steal property, issue threats of violence, and in some cases, act on these threats.
- Displays intense hostility and resentment ("venom") toward the targeted parent.
- Typically behaves well with all other adults, except those associated with the targeted parent.
- Remains emotionally distant, showing no genuine love, affection, or appreciation for the rejected parent.

73

- Lacks shame or guilt for mistreating the targeted parent.
- Develops a strong, irrational aversion toward the rejected parent, despite having previously shared a close bond—this aversion may manifest as fear, hatred, or both.
- Shows no signs of critical thinking, blindly accepting negative narratives about the targeted parent.
- Engages in "hatred by association"—extending hostility to people, objects, or even pets connected to the rejected parent.

Chapter #10: The 3 Levels of Severity of PA

Causes of Parental Alienation

Parental alienation (PA) occurs when one parent manipulates a child to reject the other parent without legitimate justification. This behavior is often driven by psychological, emotional, and situational factors. Below are key causes and triggers of PA, supported by evidence and expert insights:

- **High-Conflict Divorce or Separation**
  - Contentious custody battles and prolonged legal disputes create an environment where one parent may use alienation as a strategy to gain control.
  - Parental alienation frequently occurs in contentious divorces, where one parent attempts to eliminate the other from the child's life entirely (Harman et al., 2019).
- **Personality Disorders in the Alienating Parent**
  - Narcissistic, borderline, or antisocial traits in a parent can drive manipulative behaviors and a need for control.
  - Alienating parents often display characteristics associated with narcissistic personality disorder, viewing their child not as a separate individual, but as a reflection or extension of their own identity (Baker & Eichler, 2016).
- **Unresolved Anger and Emotional Resentment**
  - A parent who feels wronged—whether by infidelity, financial disputes, or emotional betrayal—may seek revenge by turning the child against the other parent.
  - Alienating parents frequently rely on past conflicts to rationalize their behavior, channeling unresolved resentment through the child and shaping a distorted view of the targeted parent (Baker & Eichler, 2016).

- **Lack of Boundaries Between Parent and Child (Enmeshment)**
  - The alienating parent treats the child as a confidant, exposing them to adult conflicts and personal grievances.
  - In enmeshed relationships, the alienating parent creates an unhealthy emotional bond that stifles the child's autonomy and discourages independent thought (Harman & Biringnen, 2016).
- **Fear of Losing the Child's Affection**
  - Some parents, consciously or unconsciously, fear that the child may favor the other parent and seek to "secure" their loyalty through alienation tactics.
  - Alienating parents may resort to psychological manipulation out of fear that their child's affection is not secure, perceiving any closeness with the other parent as a threat to their own relationship with the child (Harman & Biringen, 2016).
- **Extended Family and Social Reinforcement (aka Flying Monkeys)**
  - Grandparents, new spouses, or friends who support the alienating parent's narrative may reinforce negative perceptions of the rejected parent.
  - Children who experience alienation are frequently exposed to harmful narratives not just from the alienating parent but also from others in their social circle, such as relatives, friends, or community members (Baker, 2007).
- **Legal and Institutional Failures**
  - Courts and therapists unfamiliar with PA may fail to recognize manipulation, inadvertently supporting the alienating parent's claims.
  - **Professionals without proper training may inadvertently support the alienation process by misinterpreting a child's unjustified rejection of a parent as warranted estrangement** (Harman & Lorandos, 2021).

- **Revenge**
  - A parent might resort to alienation as a way to retaliate against the other parent for perceived betrayals, like infidelity or the end of the relationship.
  - Parental alienation often stems from a deep-seated need for retaliation, where the alienating parent weaponizes the child to inflict emotional pain on the targeted parent (Harman et al., 2018).
- **Self-Righteousness**
  - The alienating parent may genuinely believe they are protecting the child from harm, even in the absence of any abuse or neglect.
  - Alienating parents frequently view themselves as virtuous defenders, believing their actions are warranted—even when there is no real threat. This skewed mindset causes them to depict the other parent as harmful, even when the facts do not support such claims (Harman & Biringen, 2016).
- **Fear of Losing the Child**
  - The alienating parent may worry that the child will prefer the other parent and work to ensure the child's loyalty through manipulation.
  - The fear of abandonment is a strong motivator for alienation, prompting parents to foster dependency while encouraging rejection of the other parent (Baker & Eichler, 2016).
- **Sense of Past History**
  - Past grievances, such as childhood trauma or failed relationships, may influence a parent's decision to alienate the other parent.
  - Parents who have unresolved trauma from their own past experiences or previous relationships may transfer their fear

and anxieties onto their co-parent, using alienating behaviors as a defense mechanism (Harman & Biringen, 2016).

- **Proprietary Perspective**
  - The alienating parent may see the child as their possession, feeling entitled to exclusive control.
  - Some parents believe that because they gave birth to or raised the child, they have exclusive control over the child's upbringing and relationships (Harman & Lorandos, 2021).
- **Jealousy**
  - Feelings of jealousy—either of the child's affection for the targeted parent or of the targeted parent's new relationships—can fuel alienation.
  - An alienating parent may feel threatened by the child's connection with the other parent and try to undermine it, seeing the relationship as a challenge to their own emotional stability or authority (Baker & Eichler, 2016).
- **Child Support**
  - Financial obligations may motivate a parent to alienate the child to reduce or eliminate support payments.
  - Some parents may try to manipulate custody arrangements and turn the child against the other parent in an effort to avoid or minimize child support responsibilities, using the child as leverage in financial conflicts (Harman & Biringen, 2016).
- **Loss of Identity**
  - The alienating parent may tie their sense of self-worth to their role as the primary caregiver, feeling threatened by the child's relationship with the other parent.
  - For some parents, engaging in alienation becomes a defense mechanism to preserve their identity and shield themselves from feelings of insecurity (Baker, 2007).

- **Out of Sight, Out of Mind**
  - When the targeted parent is physically absent—whether due to relocation, job demands, or other commitments—the alienating parent may exploit this gap to diminish or eliminate the child's emotional connection to them.
  - If a parent is physically absent due to relocation or other factors, the remaining parent might exploit this distance to erode the child's relationship with the absent parent, leading the child to believe that the other parent is irrelevant or no longer plays a meaningful role in their life (Baker & Eichler, 2016).
- **Self-Protection**
  - The alienating parent may fear exposure of his/her own negative behaviors (e.g., substance abuse, emotional instability) and attempt to vilify the other parent as a distraction.
  - An alienating parent often deflects their own flaws onto the targeted parent, seeking to maintain an illusion of moral superiority (Harman et al., 2018).
- **Maintaining the Marital/Adult Relationship Through Conflict**
  - Some alienating parents use the child as a means to continue engaging with their ex-partner, keeping them emotionally entangled.
  - For some alienating parents, the prolonged conflict acts as a method to retain a connection with their former partner, using the child as a bridge to sustain emotional ties long after the relationship has ended (Harman et al., 2016).
- **Power, Influence, Control & Domination**
  - Alienation is often about power; the alienating parent may feel empowered by dictating the child's relationships.
  - Parental alienation is a type of coercive control in which the alienating parent seeks to dominate both the child and the targeted parent (Harman & Lorandos, 2021).

Chapter #11: Causes of PA

Results of One Study Linking PA to PM

What a Study of 361 Adults Who Were Alienated as Children Revealed:

Purpose of Study:
Determine the Relationship Between Exposure to PA at Different Developmental Time Periods & Psychological Maltreatment (PM)

3 developmental periods
were studied:
ages 0-7
ages 8-12
ages 13-18

Findings found in Verrocchio et al, (2017) in *Adult report of childhood exposure to parental alienation at different developmental time periods:*

- **#1: Once parental alienation was started by a parent, it was highly unlikely to stop.**
  - This implies that mental health and legal professionals should be cautious about giving repeated chances to parents who engage in these behaviors without applying appropriate consequences or incentives.
  - Considering the harmful impact of parental alienation (PA) on children and its strong correlation with psychological maltreatment, stronger enforcement and more consistent consequences are likely necessary for those found to be engaging in such conduct. This recommendation is supported by a recent review (as cited in Templer, Matthewson, Haines, & Cox, 2017), which found that **therapeutic interventions paired with court-imposed sanctions for non-compliance are the most effective approach to addressing parental alienation.**

- **#2: New instances of parental alienation (PA) were identified across all three developmental stages studied.** This indicates that even if a parent has not previously exhibited alienating behaviors, it does not guarantee they won't begin doing so in the future.

- **#3: A parent should never assume that just because parental alienation hasn't occurred yet, it won't begin at some point in the future.**

- **#4: Parents tend to use different parental alienation (PA) strategies depending on the child's developmental stage.** Tactics like confiding in the child or asking them to keep secrets often appear later, as these require more advanced cognitive and emotional abilities. This pattern suggests that parents may be adjusting their alienating behaviors based on the child's level of maturity. If this is true, then interventions aimed at preventing or addressing alienation must also be developmentally appropriate—designed to match the child's age and stage of development—and should recognize that the specific alienating tactics used may evolve over time.

- **#5: There was a statistically significant link between parental alienation (PA) and children's self-reports of experiencing psychological maltreatment (PM).**

81
Chapter #12: Linking PA to PM

Chapter #13: DSM-5 Codes & PA

PA & DSM-5
DIAGNOSIS

Parental Alienation __IS NOT__ currently listed in the DSM-5 however listed below are diagnoses & codes that can be used in support of PA.

1. Adjustment Disorder (85)
Code: 309.X / DSM-5 / p. 286-287

2. Child Affected by Parental Relationship Distress (87)
(CAPRD)   Code: V61.29 / DSM-5 / p.716

3. Child Neglect (89)
Code: 995.92 / DSM-5 / pp.718-719

4. Child Psychological Abuse (91)
Code: 995.51 / DSM-5 / p.719

5. Educational Problems (95)
Code: V62.3 / DSM-5 / p.723

6. Factitious Disorder (97)
Code: 300.19 / DSM-5 / pp. 324-325

7. High Expressed Emotion Level Within Family (99)
Code: V61.8 / DSM-5 / p.716

8. Parent Child Relational Problem (101)
Code: V62.10 / DSM-5 / p.715

(Diagnostic and Statistical Manual of Mental Disorders: APA, 2013)

Chapter #13: DSM-5 Codes & PA

1. Adjustment Disorder
Code: 309.X / DSM-5 / p. 286-287

According to the *Diagnostic and Statistical Manual of Mental Disorders* (5th ed.; DSM-5: American Psychiatric Association, 2013):

Adjustment disorder is characterized by emotional or behavioral responses to a specific stressor, usually occurring within three months of its onset. These reactions cause significant distress that exceeds the intensity of the stressor or result in considerable difficulties in areas such as social, professional, or daily functioning. It differs from normal grieving and typically improves within six months once the stressor or its effects have concluded.

Adjustment Disorder and Parental Alienation

Adjustment disorder arises when a person struggles to cope with a significant life stressor, resulting in emotional or behavioral symptoms that interfere with daily life. In the context of parental alienation, children exposed to ongoing psychological manipulation, conflict, and the forced absence of a parent may experience this disorder. The emotional turmoil caused by being caught in the middle of divided loyalties can lead to marked distress and difficulties in functioning.

How Parental Alienation Contributes to Adjustment Disorder

- **Severe Emotional Distress:** The stress of being manipulated into rejecting a loving parent can overwhelm a child's coping mechanisms, leading to adjustment disorder symptoms such as anxiety, depression, and behavioral disturbances (APA, 2013).
- **Impaired Social and Emotional Functioning:** Children affected by parental alienation often face academic challenges, strained peer relationships, and an inability to trust others—symptoms that closely reflect those outlined in the DSM-5 criteria for adjustment disorder.

These emotional and social difficulties are frequently triggered by the chronic stress and instability caused by the alienation dynamic (APA, 2013).

- **Maladaptive Coping Mechanisms:** In response to alienation, children may develop unhealthy ways of dealing with stress, such as aggression, withdrawal, or defiance, further supporting the link between parental alienation and adjustment disorder (Lorandos et al., 2013).
- **Long-Term Psychological Consequences:** Studies indicate that unresolved adjustment disorder in alienated children can evolve into more severe mental health conditions, including depression and anxiety disorders, reinforcing the need for early intervention (Lorandos et al., 2013).

Parental alienation acts as a significant stressor, making children highly susceptible to adjustment disorder. Recognizing this link is crucial for mental health professionals in diagnosing and treating affected children.

2. Child Affected by Parental Relationship Distress
(CAPRD) Code: V61.29 / DSM-5 / p.716

According to the *Diagnostic and Statistical Manual of Mental Disorders* (5th ed.; DSM-5: American Psychiatric Association, 2013):

This diagnostic category is intended for situations where a child's emotional or physical well-being is adversely affected by ongoing parental conflict—such as frequent arguments, emotional tension, or verbal denigration. The focus is on how this discord contributes to or exacerbates mental health challenges or other medical issues in the child.

CAPRD & Parental Alienation

"Parental alienation specialists have argued that severe parental alienating behaviors (PABs) are a form of child abuse (as cited in Templar et al., 2017)**, and severe parental alienation is an extreme manifestation of both CARPD and "parent-child relational problem" in the *DSM–5*."** (Harman et al., 2018)

According to Harman et al. (2018) in *Parental Alienating Behaviors: An Unacknowledged Form of Family Violence*, the Child Affected by Parental Relationship Distress (CAPRD) category encompasses a spectrum of harmful parental dynamics, including high-conflict relationships, intimate partner violence, and parental alienation. These behaviors represent a significant, yet often overlooked, form of family violence that can severely impact a child's development and well-being. Research shows that chronic exposure to parental conflict and psychological aggression increases a child's risk of emotional dysregulation, academic struggles, social difficulties, and behavioral disorders (as cited in Amato, 2001; Douglas & Hines, 2016a, 2016b).

The CAPRD framework underscores how children may become enmeshed in various degrees of parental discord, from mild disputes to emotionally abusive or coercively controlling dynamics. This repeated exposure can result in psychological trauma and an elevated risk of long-term mental health challenges (as cited in Brock & Kochanska, 2016; Koss et al., 2013; Wozencraft et al., 2019).

When parents involve children in their interpersonal battles—whether directly or indirectly—the child may experience intense loyalty conflicts (as cited in Hetherington, 1999) or feel compelled to reject one parent entirely, often as a result of subtle or overt psychological manipulation (as cited in Bernet et al., 2016). In more severe cases, this manipulation stems from patterns of coercive control, similar to what is described in the literature as "intimate terrorism" (as cited in Johnson, 2008), where emotional abuse and domination are used to damage the child's relationship with the other parent.

Chapter #13: DSM-5 Codes & PA

3. Child Neglect
Code: 995.92 / DSM-5 / pp.718-719

According to the *Diagnostic and Statistical Manual of Mental Disorders* (5th ed.; DSM-5: American Psychiatric Association, 2013):

Child neglect refers to any verified or suspected severe act or omission by a parent or caregiver that denies a child essential age-appropriate needs, leading to actual or potential physical or psychological harm. This form of neglect includes abandonment, inadequate supervision, failure to meet emotional or psychological needs, and neglecting to provide essential education, medical care, nutrition, shelter, or clothing.

Child Neglect & Parental Alienation

"Neglect is a fundamental element of parental alienation because the [Alienating Parent's (AP)] needs are placed ahead of those of the child, and the AP fails to recognize the need for the child to be loved and cared for by the [Target Parent (TP)]." (Harman et al., 2018)

As described by Harman et al. (2018) *Parental Alienating Behaviors: An Unacknowledged Form of Family Violence*, alienating parents (APs) often establish a psychologically contradictory environment in which children are simultaneously infantilized—treated as helpless and entirely dependent—and parentified, expected to assume roles and responsibilities beyond their developmental capabilities. This dual manipulation reflects a profound neglect of the child's psychological and emotional needs, prioritizing control over genuine caregiving (as cited in Johnston, Walters, & Olesen, 2005).

Many APs pursue sole custody not with the child's well-being in mind, but as a means to dominate and punish the targeted parent (TP), using the child as leverage in a broader campaign of coercive control (as cited in Baker, 2006b). Rather than fostering a healthy parent-child bond, APs may delegate parenting duties to third-party caregivers, while remaining emotionally disengaged due to unresolved psychological issues (as cited Garber, 2011; Harman & Biringen, 2016).

This strategy of emotional and relational manipulation severs the child's connection with a loving and supportive parent, robbing them of critical emotional stability. Over time, the resulting psychological harm may manifest as chronic anxiety, depression, and significant difficulties in forming secure, healthy relationships (Harman et al., 2018).

4. Child Psychological Abuse
Code: 995.51 / DSM-5 / p.719

(Physical and sexual abusive acts are not included in this category.)
According to the *Diagnostic and Statistical Manual of Mental Disorders* (5th ed.; DSM-5: American Psychiatric Association, 2013):

Child psychological abuse involves deliberate verbal or symbolic actions by a parent or caregiver that cause, or are likely to cause, significant psychological harm to the child.

Examples of psychological abuse of a child include:

Psychological maltreatment of children encompasses various harmful behaviors by caregivers that can severely impact a child's emotional and psychological well-being. These behaviors include:

- Berating, disparaging, or humiliating the child
- Threatening the child
- Harming/abandoning the child
- Indicating intent to harm people or things the child cares about like material objects
- Confining the child to a space or using physical means to do so
- Scapegoating by blaming the child for problems, failures, break-ups
- Coercing the child to inflict self-pain
- Using excessive discipline by physical or non-physical means

(APA, 2013)

Child Psychological Abuse & Parental Alienation

As outlined in Harman et al., (2018), *Parental Alienating Behaviors: An Unacknowledged Form of Family Violence:*

Alienating parents (APs) use a variety of coercive strategies to erode a child's relationship with the targeted parent (TP), often portraying the TP as unsafe, unloving, or unworthy. This manipulation instills fear, confusion, and emotional distress, leading the child to unjustifiably reject the TP. Studies have shown that APs disparage the TP in front of the child, reinforcing the belief that any affection toward the TP is dangerous or disloyal (as cited in Baker & Verrocchio, 2013; Verrocchio et al., 2017).

Emotional coercion is frequently used to sever the parent-child bond. Children may be shamed, rejected, or guilted for expressing positive feelings toward the TP (as cited in Harman & Biringen, 2018; Baker & Darnall, 2006), and even displays of warmth can be ridiculed (as cited in López et al., 2014). To avoid the AP's disapproval, the child often suppresses their emotional needs or adopts a split identity—behaving differently with each parent (as cited in Garber, 2014; Dunne & Hedrick, 1994).

Love withdrawal is another tactic: APs may withhold affection or express disappointment when a child mentions the TP positively (as cited in Baker & Verrocchio, 2015). Over time, the child learns that emotional safety depends on rejecting the TP.

Alienating behavior also includes rewarding acts of rejection—such as ignoring the TP in public—or using demeaning labels for them (as cited in Warshak, 2015b; López et al., 2014). APs often monitor communication, interrogate children about time spent with the TP, and destroy keepsakes or gifts, further dismantling emotional bonds (as cited in Baker & Darnall, 2006; Harman & Biringen, 2018).

In extreme cases, APs attempt to erase the TP's presence altogether—encouraging children to refer to another adult as "mom" or "dad," altering surnames, or performing symbolic acts like mock funerals to represent the TP's removal from the child's life (as cited in Warshak, 2015c; Dunne & Hedrick, 1994).

Boundary violations and secrecy also play a role. APs may blur parent-child roles by encouraging the child to use first names or keep secrets from the TP (as cited in Harman & Biringen, 2018; Reay, 2011).

Gaslighting—manipulating the child into questioning their reality—is another common tactic. APs may distort memories, fabricate abuse, or imply the TP abandoned them, fostering long-term confusion and mistrust (as cited in Reay, 2011; Warshak, 2015a).

Misinformation is frequently used to sabotage the parent-child relationship. For example, APs might falsely claim that the TP missed a visit or "forgot" about the child (as cited in Lorandos, 2013; Harman & Biringen, 2018). These lies deepen the child's sense of rejection while bolstering loyalty to the AP.

Loyalty conflicts are deliberately fostered, pressuring the child to choose sides (as cited in Verrocchio et al., 2017). In some cases, children are enlisted as spies, asked to gather personal information from the TP or report on their behavior (as cited in Baker & Verrocchio, 2013; Stahl, 2004).

Another damaging tactic is parentification—placing the child in adult roles, such as managing the AP's emotional needs, legal matters, or household responsibilities (as cited in Moné & Biringen, 2012; Balmer et al., 2017). This role reversal deepens the child's entanglement in the conflict and reinforces dependence on the AP.

Finally, APs often frame visitation with the TP as a "choice," saying things like, "I can't force them to go," while subtly encouraging the child to reject contact (as cited in Baker & Darnall, 2006; Warshak, 2015). Adolescents, in particular, are vulnerable to this manipulation due to their developmental stage and desire for autonomy.

These cumulative tactics systematically dismantle a child's relationship with the TP, leaving deep psychological wounds. Harman et al. (2018) emphasizes that understanding these behaviors is essential to identifying and intervening in cases of parental alienation—a form of family violence that often goes unrecognized but has devastating long-term effects.

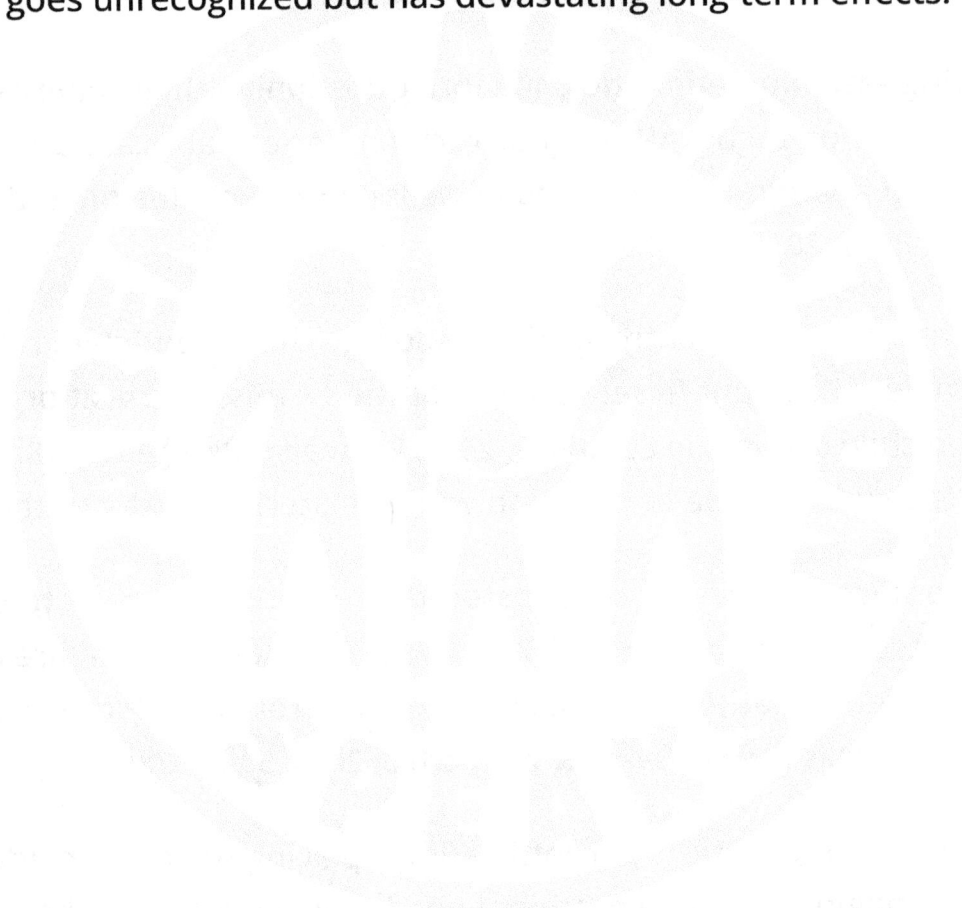

5. Educational Problems
Code: V62.3 / DSM-5 / p.723

According to the *Diagnostic and Statistical Manual of Mental Disorders* (5th ed.; DSM-5: American Psychiatric Association, 2013):

This category is designated when academic or educational issues warrant clinical attention or significantly affect an individual's diagnosis, treatment, or prognosis. Such issues include illiteracy or limited literacy skills; lack of access to education due to unavailability or unattainability; challenges in academic performance, such as failing exams or receiving poor grades; underachievement relative to the individual's intellectual capabilities; conflicts with teachers, school staff, or peers; and other problems related to education and literacy.

Educational Problems & Parental Alienation

According to Harman et al. (2018) in *Parental Alienating Behaviors: An Unacknowledged Form of Family Violence*, targeted parents (TPs) have reported that alienating parents (APs) neglect their children's academic needs by permitting frequent school absences for appointments that could be scheduled outside school hours. By appearing preoccupied with addressing the children's "complex" needs, APs project an image of being the more concerned and competent parent, while, in reality, the children's genuine needs remain unmet.

96

6. Factitious Disorder Imposed on Another (FDIA)
Code: 300.19 / DSM-5 / pp. 324-325

*The information in the DSM-5 is extensive. Please go to page 325 of the DSM-5 for all information.

According to the *Diagnostic and Statistical Manual of Mental Disorders* (5th ed.; DSM-5: American Psychiatric Association, 2013):

Factitious Disorder Imposed on Another (FDIA), formerly known as Munchausen Syndrome by Proxy, is a serious form of child neglect in which an individual, typically a caregiver, deliberately fabricates, exaggerates, or induces medical or psychological symptoms in another person, usually a child or dependent, to gain attention or sympathy.

Key Characteristics of FDIA:

- The perpetrator creates or falsifies medical conditions in another person.
- The victim is subjected to unnecessary medical treatments or interventions.
- The perpetrator often appears deeply concerned about the victim's health, presenting themselves as a devoted caregiver.
- Symptoms cease when the victim is removed from the perpetrator's care
- The perpetrator (alienator) receives the diagnosis, not the victim (child)

(APA, 2013, pp. 324-325)

Factitious Disorder & Parental Alienation

According to Harman et al. (2018) in *Parental Alienating Behaviors: An Unacknowledged Form of Family Violence*, Factitious Disorder Imposed on Another (FDIA) can overlap with parental alienation when one parent deceitfully portrays their child as physically or psychologically unwell to influence custody decisions or weaken the child's bond with the other parent. This manipulation can inflict significant psychological harm on the child, fostering emotional dependence on the alienating parent and distancing them from the targeted parent. Such behavior enables the alienating parent to exploit medical concerns as a means of control and to discredit the targeted parent.

Research indicates that FDIA is more prevalent among mothers with a history of abuse and personality disorders, such as borderline personality disorder, with abusive behaviors intensifying during periods of separation from the child (as cited in Yates & Bass, 2017) . In instances of parental alienation, alienating parents may fabricate or exaggerate medical issues to justify restricting the targeted parent's involvement, alleging that the targeted parent is incapable of providing appropriate care.

Alienating parents (APs) may deliberately provide the targeted parent (TP) with false medical information regarding their child's condition or treatment. When the TP does not adhere to these misleading instructions, the AP may harass them and assert to the children that only they (the AP) are capable of meeting their needs. This behavior not only isolates the child from the TP but also fosters a dependency on the AP, reinforcing the alienation. Furthermore, APs often appear preoccupied with addressing the 'complex' needs of the children, creating an illusion of being the more concerned and competent parent while actually neglecting the child's true needs.

7. <u>High Expressed Emotion (EE) Level Within Family</u>
Code: V61.8 / DSM-5 / p.716

According to the *Diagnostic and Statistical Manual of Mental Disorders* (5th ed.; DSM-5: American Psychiatric Association, 2013):

High Expressed Emotion (EE) is a concept that quantifies the level of emotion, particularly hostility, emotional overinvolvement, and criticism, directed at a family member who is considered the identified patient. It is relevant when the high level of expressed emotion within the family is central to clinical focus or is influencing the development, outlook, or treatment of a family member's mental or physical health condition.

<u>High Expressed Emotion (EE) Level Within Family & PA</u>

According to Harman et al. (2018) in *Parental Alienating Behaviors: An Unacknowledged Form of Family Violence*, High Expressed Emotion Level Within Family is closely related to parental alienation as it reflects the high levels of hostility, criticism, and emotional over-involvement commonly present in alienating family dynamics.

In parental alienation, the alienating parent often engages in behaviors like criticizing the targeted parent, manipulating the child's emotions, and creating an atmosphere of fear and rejection. Research shows that children exposed to these high EE environments are at a greater risk of developing emotional instability, anxiety, and depression.

Additionally, alienated children often reflect the alienating parent's intense emotions, showing baseless hostility and disdain directed at the rejected parent. This pattern perpetuates the alienation and exacerbates the psychological damage to the child. Recognizing the impact of high EE in parental alienation helps mental health professionals more effectively evaluate and address the emotional manipulation central to this form of psychological abuse.

Chapter #13: DSM-5 Codes & PA

8. Parent Child Relational Problem
Code: V62.10 / DSM-5 / p.715

According to the *Diagnostic and Statistical Manual of Mental Disorders* (5th ed.; DSM-5: American Psychiatric Association, 2013):

"Parent" encompasses any primary caregiver responsible for a child's well-being, including biological, adoptive, or foster parents, as well as relatives like grandparents who fulfill a parental role. This classification is pertinent when clinical intervention focuses on the parent-child relationship or when difficulties within this relationship affect the diagnosis, treatment, or prognosis of a mental or medical disorder. Such relational issues often present as impairments in behavioral, cognitive, or emotional functioning.

Examples of Parent-Child Relational Problems:

Behavioral Issues:

- Insufficient parental guidance and engagement
- Excessive parental shielding
- Overbearing parental expectations
- Escalating conflicts leading to threats of physical violence
- Avoidance of issues without resolution
  (APA, 2013)

Cognitive Issues:

- Negative assumptions about the other's intentions
- Hostility, scapegoating, or assigning blame unfairly
- Unjustified feelings of estrangement
  (APA, 2013)

Emotional Issues:

- Persistent sadness, apathy, or anger toward the other person in the relationship

(APA, 2013)

Clinicians should consider the child's developmental needs and cultural background when assessing and addressing parent-child relational difficulties (APA, 2013).

Parent-Child Relational Problem & PA

According to Harman et al. (2018) in *Parental Alienating Behaviors: An Unacknowledged Form of Family Violence*, alienating parents (AP) deliberately interfere with a child's ability to maintain a meaningful relationship with the targeted parent, often resulting in unjustified fear, anger, or rejection. This manipulative dynamic reflects the criteria for a Parent-Child Relational Problem, as outlined in the DSM-5, by fostering an environment in which the child internalizes distorted beliefs about the alienated parent. These false narratives contribute to escalating emotional conflict and a growing sense of detachment within the parent-child bond.

Alienated children frequently adopt rigid, negative perceptions of the targeted parent, even in cases where the relationship was previously warm and secure (as cited in Bernet et al., 2016). This deterioration in the relationship can lead to a complete refusal of contact, highlighting the depth of the psychological rupture.

The long-term effects of such alienation are profound. Children subjected to these dynamics often struggle with anxiety, depression, and identity confusion, as their emotional development is shaped by ongoing loyalty conflicts and coercive psychological control. Given these damaging outcomes, parental alienation clearly aligns with the diagnostic framework of a Parent-Child Relational Problem, as it significantly impairs healthy attachment and compromises the child's emotional and psychological well-being.

Chapter #13: DSM-5 Codes & PA

Chapter #13: DSM-5 Codes & PA

ACES and Parental Alienation

The **Adverse Childhood Experiences (ACE) Study**, a joint effort by Kaiser Permanente and the Centers for Disease Control and Prevention, examined how early life trauma can impact health and well-being later in life (Chadwick et al., 2014, p. 224). More than 17,000 participants completed surveys evaluating eight forms of adversity during childhood, including emotional, physical, and sexual abuse; witnessing domestic violence; living with a parent or household member suffering from mental illness or substance abuse; experiencing parental divorce or separation; and having an incarcerated family member (Chadwick et al., 2014, p. 224).

Findings revealed a strong correlation between the number of ACEs and negative health outcomes. Also, **the higher the ACES score, the higher the likelihood of psychological and physical issues** (Chadwick et al., 2014, p.224). For instance, adults with four ACEs were four times more likely to have attempted suicide, while those with seven or more ACEs faced a 17-fold increase in risk (Chadwick et al., 2014, p.224).

ACEs and Their Psychological Impact

Although the Adverse Childhood Experiences (ACEs) study doesn't specifically mention parental alienation, it would easily fall under **emotional abuse, emotional neglect and household dysfunction**.

ACEs are closely connected to a variety of lasting mental, emotional, and physical health problems, such as:

- Persistent anxiety and depressive symptoms
- Poor self-image and low confidence
- Higher likelihood of substance misuse
- Challenges in building and sustaining relationships
- Suicidal thoughts or tendencies

Chapter #14: ACES & PA

(Chadwick et al., 2014, p.224).

Children experiencing PA often accumulate multiple ACEs, compounding their trauma and risk factors for future emotional distress.

PA as an ACE: How It Meets the Criteria (+3 ACES)

- **Emotional Abuse (+1):** Alienating parents manipulate, gaslight, and emotionally coerce the child into rejecting the target parent, causing confusion and emotional distress.
- **Emotional Neglect (+1):** The alienator often discourages independent thought, making the child emotionally dependent and suppressing their authentic emotions. Alienators will often shun and ignore a child when showing positive emotions for the TP.
- **Exposure to Household Dysfunction:** Alienated children often live in high-conflict, unstable environments where they experience chronic stress and insecurity.
  - **Parental Separation (+1):** PA exacerbates the trauma of divorce or separation by forcing the child to take sides and reject a once-loved parent.

Some of the Psychological Consequences of PA in Relation to ACEs:

- **Cognitive Dissonance & Identity Struggles**
  - Children internalize false narratives about the target parent, leading to confusion about their own identity and self-worth.
  - Children who experience alienation often have trouble developing a clear sense of self, as they are caught between opposing and confusing messages about their family and personal history (Baker, 2007).

Chapter #14: ACES & PA

- **PTSD and Complex Trauma**
  - Constant exposure to a hostile environment causes hyper-vigilance, emotional numbness, and difficulty forming secure attachments.
- **Depression and Anxiety**
  - Alienated children often experience psychological distress similar to that of abuse or neglect, feeling caught between loyalty conflicts and overwhelming fear (Harman et al., 2022).
- **Insecure Attachment and Future Relationships**
  - Alienated children struggle with trust and intimacy, often replicating toxic relational patterns into adulthood.
  - PA has been compared to "coercive control," a tactic commonly used in domestic abuse cases (Harman et al., 2018).

Breaking the Cycle: Recognizing PA as an ACE

- Educating professionals (therapists, social workers, legal professionals) about the link between PA and ACEs is crucial for early intervention.
- Legal and therapeutic interventions should focus on removing children from emotionally abusive environments and restoring their autonomy.
- Trauma-informed approaches in therapy can help children process their experiences and rebuild healthy relationships with both parents when parental alienation is recognized early.
- Intervention should prioritize the child's well-being, ensuring they are not manipulated or caught in the middle of parental disputes (Baker & Eichler, 2016).

ACEs are ADVERSE CHILDHOOD EXPERIENCES

THE TRUTH ABOUT ACES

#1. ABUSE | #2. NEGLECT | #3. HOUSEHOLD DYSFUNCTION

CATEGORIES OF ACES

Physical

Emotional Abuse

Sexual

Emotional Neglect

Mental Illness

Incarcerated Relative

Mother treated violently

Substance Abuse

Divorce

The Higher the ACEs Score, the higher the likelihood of psychological & physical issues

Parental Alienation = +3

Possible Outcomes:

BEHAVIOR

Lack of physical activity | Smoking | Alcoholism | Drug use | Missed work

PHYSICAL & MENTAL HEALTH

Severe obesity | Diabetes | Depression | Suicide attempts | STDs

Heart disease | Cancer | Stroke | COPD | Broken bones

WHAT IMPACT DO ACEs HAVE?

HIGH RISK

LOW RISK

?? HOW MANY ACES OUT OF A SCORE OF 10 ??

Adverse childhood experiences (aces). RWJF. (2025). https://www.rwjf.org/en/insights/collections/adverse-childhood-experiences.html

108

Sinister Tactics Used By An Alienator

1. Physically Aggressive Behavior Toward the Targeted Parent

- Alienated children may become unusually aggressive toward the TP, displaying behaviors such as hitting, yelling, or even destroying property (Baker, 2007).
- Their aggression often lacks a rational basis and mirrors the AP's negative rhetoric about the TP (Harman et al., 2019).
- The child may claim they are "defending themselves" against an imagined threat, reinforcing the false belief that the TP is harmful (Verrocchio et al., 2016).
- This aggression is often out of proportion to any prior interactions, reflecting the internalized belief that the TP is dangerous or unworthy (Harman et al., 2019).
- The child may justify their aggression by echoing the AP's false accusations, such as "You deserve this because you abandoned me" or "You are dangerous" (Verrocchio et al., 2016).
- Research suggests that alienated children adopt these behaviors as a means of securing the AP's approval and demonstrating loyalty (Baker & Darnall, 2006).

2. "Disappearing" in Public Places to Disrupt Time with the TP

- Alienated children may hide in stores, parks, or other public settings to avoid spending time with the TP, forcing the parent to search for them instead of bonding (Harman et al., 2019).
- This behavior creates stress and frustration for the TP while reinforcing the child's belief that time with them is undesirable.

- This tactic serves multiple functions: it increases the TP's frustration, reinforces the narrative that spending time with them is unpleasant, and can be reported back to the AP as proof of a negative visit.
- The child may later distort the event to the AP, portraying the TP as inattentive or irresponsible (Warshak, 2010).
- Some children may use these avoidance behaviors as a subconscious method of aligning with the AP's expectations, reinforcing the belief that time with the TP is unwanted or unsafe (Warshak, 2010).
- Disappearing acts can also be a way for children to regain a sense of control in a situation where they feel torn between their parents (Baker, 2007).

3. Pathological Lying About the Targeted Parent

- Alienated children frequently fabricate stories about the TP, making false claims of neglect or mistreatment that align with the AP's narrative (Harman et al., 2019).
- These lies are often delivered with conviction, showing no signs of guilt, hesitation, or self-correction—hallmarks of indoctrination rather than personal experience (Baker & Verrocchio, 2016).
- Over time, these false accusations can escalate, leading to serious legal and psychological consequences for the TP (Verrocchio et al., 2016).

4. Sudden and Unexplained Affective Changes

- The alienated child may display abrupt mood swings when interacting with the TP, showing affection one moment and hostility the next (Baker & Darnall, 2006).
- Emotional responses may seem rehearsed, as if the child is performing for the AP's approval (Harman et al., 2019).

5. A Sense of Entitlement Toward the Targeted Parent

- Alienated children may develop an exaggerated sense of entitlement, demanding excessive favors, gifts, or privileges from the TP while showing little to no gratitude (Baker, 2007).
- They may feel justified in treating the TP with disrespect, refusing to follow rules, or rejecting parental authority outright (Harman et al., 2019).
- This entitlement is often fueled by the AP's reinforcement that the TP "owes" the child something due to perceived past wrongs (Warshak, 2010).
- If the TP does not comply with these demands, the child may respond with anger, withdrawal, or further rejection, reinforcing the alienation dynamic (Baker & Darnall, 2006).

6. Braces and Dental Care as a Control Tactic
Alienating parents may employ various tactics to control or restrict the targeted parent's (TP) involvement in their child's life, particularly concerning medical treatments like orthodontic care:

- **Exclusive Management of Medical Appointments:** The alienating parent might insist that only *they* can handle the child's medical appointments, claiming that their exclusive involvement is necessary for the child's well-being (Baker, 2007).

- **Scheduling Conflicts:** They may arrange treatment schedules that overlap with the TP's visitation times, using the child's medical needs as a reason to limit contact (Baker, 2007).
- **Dietary Restrictions:** Under the guise of protecting the child's braces, the alienating parent could instruct the child to avoid certain foods while with the TP, creating additional stress and division (Harman et al., 2019).

Chapter #15: Sinister Tactics Used By An Alienator

- **Undermining the TP's Care:** These tactics can reinforce the belief that the TP is neglectful or incapable of properly caring for the child's needs, further alienating the child from the TP (Lorandos et al., 2013).

These behaviors not only hinder the TP's relationship with their child but also serve as a means for the alienating parent to exert control over the TP, potentially leading to financial and emotional strain.

7. Haircuts as a Manipulation Tool

Alienating parents may use haircuts as a method of control to undermine the targeted parent's (TP) involvement and influence. Specific tactics include:

- Scheduling haircuts immediately before or after the child's visits with the TP to assert dominance over the child's appearance and signal the TP's lack of influence (Baker, 2007).
- Convincing the child to resist grooming or styling changes suggested by the TP, reinforcing the notion that the TP has no say in the child's life (Harman et al., 2019).
- Using drastic haircuts as a form of punishment or reward, controlling the child's self-image and fostering dependency on the alienating parent for approval (Lorandos et al., 2013).
- These tactics serve to create stress and division, portraying the TP as neglectful or incapable of properly caring for the child's needs.

8. Murder

Child custody disputes can escalate to tragic outcomes, including instances of murder. Notable cases include:

-Taylor Santiago's Alleged Murder Spree (2025): In a harrowing case that spans two states and highlights the potential for violence in high-conflict custody disputes, Taylor Santiago of Missouri allegedly carried out a deadly series of attacks against two former partners. According to the *New York*

Post (Janoski, 2025), Santiago is accused of fatally shooting her estranged husband, Troy Huffman, before driving across state lines to Arkansas, where she allegedly shot her ex-boyfriend, Nathan Green, and his new girlfriend, Sophia Williams. Williams and Huffman were both killed in the attacks.

Investigators believe the motive behind these violent acts was rooted in ongoing custody battles Santiago had with both men. The article notes that tensions had been escalating, and Santiago ultimately turned herself in to authorities, now facing multiple charges, including murder (Janoski, 2025).

This deeply unsettling case underscores the extreme outcomes that can arise when custody disputes are fueled by rage, obsession, and unresolved emotional conflict. As described by one source in the article, "She's a monster"—a reflection of the community's shock and horror at the lengths Santiago allegedly went to in an attempt to exert control over her fractured relationships and parental rights (Janoski, 2025).

-Veronica Butler and Jilian Kelley Murders (2024): In a deeply disturbing case that has captured national attention, Veronica Butler and Jilian Kelley were tragically found deceased in a freezer in rural Oklahoma—victims of a brutal crime rooted in an alleged campaign of parental alienation. According to People.com (Staff, 2024), Tifany Adams, the children's grandmother and identified alienator, had explicitly stated in court that it would be "over her dead body" before Veronica would ever see her children again. That chilling declaration foreshadowed a horrifying outcome.

Veronica had been falsely accused of child abuse, and these allegations were used to justify court-ordered supervised visitation. Such tactics are not uncommon in severe cases of alienation, where one parent is systematically undermined and vilified in order to erase them from the child's life. As detailed in People.com (Staff, 2024), Adams's actions

Chapter #15: Sinister Tactics Used By An Alienator

extended far beyond manipulation—escalating into a calculated plan that ended in violence.

Autopsy reports confirmed that both Veronica and Jilian had sustained multiple blunt force injuries and stab wounds, suggesting that they fought desperately for their lives. The brutality of the attack highlights the potential dangers that can arise when parental alienation escalates unchecked. This tragic case stands as a stark reminder of how damaging false accusations and obsessive control over a child's relationship with their parent can become when left unchallenged (Staff, 2024).

-Sally Hill Murder (2017): In a shocking case that underscores the darkest extremes of custody battles, Eric Hill found himself at the center of a horrifying plot when his estranged wife, Rosa, and her mother, Mei Li, murdered his beloved grandmother, Sally Hill. As reported by *The Irish Sun* (Knox, 2024), the motive behind the brutal crime was chillingly strategic: Rosa and Mei aimed to frame Eric for the murder in an attempt to gain full custody of his daughter.

The couple's relationship had deteriorated into a high-conflict legal battle over custody, and what followed revealed just how far some individuals will go to eliminate the other parent. According to Knox (2024), Rosa and Mei meticulously staged the crime to implicate Eric, but police investigations ultimately uncovered the truth. Their scheme unraveled, leading to both women being found guilty and sentenced to life imprisonment.

This disturbing case illustrates how parental alienation and custody disputes can, in extreme circumstances, lead to criminal acts fueled by desperation, control, and hatred. Eric Hill's story, now the subject of growing public attention, serves as a grim reminder of how far manipulative and vindictive behavior can escalate when left unchecked (Knox, 2024).

Chapter #15: Sinister Tactics Used By An Alienator

-Derek Thebo Murder-Suicide (2021): In Lowell, Michigan, a tragic and deeply unsettling incident underscored the potentially fatal consequences of high-conflict custody disputes. Derek Thebo, during his scheduled parenting time, fatally shot his three-year-old son before turning the gun on himself. As reported by *Kraayeveld Family Law* (2024), the murder-suicide shocked the community and highlighted the devastating link between contentious custody battles, domestic violence and the lengths someone will go to in keep a child from the other parent.

This heartbreaking case is one of several noted by *Kraayeveld Family Law* (2024) that reflect a broader and deeply concerning trend—where unresolved emotional turmoil and power struggles over custody can escalate into fatal outcomes. It serves as a sobering reminder of the urgent need for mental health evaluations, risk assessments, and protective measures in family court settings where there are red flags of instability or coercive control.

Thebo's actions devastated those around him and left a permanent scar on a family already fractured by conflict—reminding professionals and parents alike of the high stakes involved in custody decisions when warning signs go unheeded.

-Cindy Crossthwaite Murder (2007): In Melbourne, Australia, the tragic case of Cindy Crossthwaite serves as a heartbreaking example of how domestic conflict, when left to spiral, can end in fatal violence. Amid a bitter custody dispute, Cindy was murdered by her estranged husband, Emil "Bill" Petrov—a man who had been charged with her death in 2019 and ultimately found guilty in December 2024 (Vallance & Silva, 2024).

As reported by *ABC News* (Vallance & Silva, 2024), the courtroom was filled with raw emotion during the pre-sentence hearing. Cindy and Emil's children delivered powerful victim impact statements, expressing their profound grief, anger, and the lasting void left by their mother's absence.

Chapter #15: Sinister Tactics Used By An Alienator

Their words painted a vivid picture of a family shattered—not just by loss, but by the trauma of violence born from a conflict that had once centered on custody and control.

This devastating case underscores the urgent need for early intervention in high-conflict custody situations, particularly when signs of coercive control or emotional abuse are present. As the Crossthwaite family mourns the loss of a "beautiful girl," as Cindy was lovingly remembered, their story stands as a sobering reminder of the stakes involved when family disputes turn dangerous (Vallance & Silva, 2024).

These cases underscore the potential for extreme violence in contentious custody disputes, emphasizing the need for vigilant legal and mental health interventions to protect those involved.

9. Financial and Legal

Alienating parents often employ financial control to manipulate and exhaust the targeted parent (TP), hindering their relationship with the child. Such tactics include:

- **Monopolizing Decision-Making:** Alienating parents may dominate choices regarding medical care, education, and extracurricular activities, limiting the TP's involvement while imposing financial burdens on them (Lorandos et al., 2013).
- **Scheduling Costly Treatments:** They might arrange expensive procedures and insist that only *they* can manage appointments, using this to disrupt the TP's visitation rights (Baker, 2007).
- **Encouraging Child's Resistance:** The alienating parent may prompt the child to reject food or necessities at the TP's home under the guise of medical concerns, portraying the TP as neglectful or incapable (Harman et al., 2019).

- **Exploiting Legal Systems:** Alienators may prolong court proceedings, file false allegations, or ignore custody agreements, compelling the TP to incur substantial legal expenses (Lorandos et al., 2013).

These strategies create a power imbalance, heightening the TP's emotional distress and diminishing their capacity to maintain a meaningful relationship with their child.

Chapter #15: Sinister Tactics Used By An Alienator

Chapter #15: Sinister Tactics Used By An Alienator

Red Flags

Red Flags for Identifying an Alienating Parent

Therapists, counselors, social workers and others play a crucial role in identifying parental alienation (PA) by recognizing behaviors that suggest psychological manipulation of the child. The following red flags may indicate a parent is actively alienating their child from the other parent:

1. Extreme Denigration of the Other Parent

- The alienating parent makes persistent negative statements about the targeted parent, portraying them as dangerous, unloving, or unfit.
- For instance:

Statements To Portray the Target Parent as Unfit:

- *"I can't believe your mom/dad took you to the lake last weekend and forgot your life jacket! How dangerous! You could've drowned!"*
- *"Your dad/mom can't even take care of himself, let alone you."*
- *"Your mom/dad doesn't even know how to cook a proper meal for you."*
- *"If the judge knew what your dad/mom was really like, you wouldn't have to go over there."*
- *"You always come back looking tired and stressed—see what I mean about him/her not being responsible?"*
- *"S/he's never been the kind of person who puts her/his children first."*
- *"You're always sick when you come home from his/her house!"*

Chapter #16: Red Flags for Identifying an Alienating Parent

Statements To Portray the Target Parent as Unloving:

- *"If your mom/dad really loved you, s/he wouldn't have left."*
- *"Your dad/mom hasn't called once this week—guess that shows how much s/he cares."*
- *"You know, your mom/dad always puts her/his new boy/girlfriend above you."*
- *"S/he only wants to see you now because s/he's trying to look good for the courts."*
- *"When you were a baby, s/he never wanted to hold you."*

Statements To Portray the Target Parent as Dangerous:

- *"Be careful when you're over there—s/he has a temper, you know."*
- *"I heard your mom/dad was drinking again... don't be alone with her/him."*
- *"Mom/Dad is an alcoholic."*
- *"If anything ever scares you at your mom/dad's, call me right away—I don't trust him/her."*
- *"S/he has mental issues, and I'm not sure it's safe for you to be there."*
- *"You never know what mood s/he's going to be in. You really shouldn't have to deal with that."*

2. Limiting or Preventing Contact

- The parent restricts the child's communication or visitation with the targeted parent, often citing excuses like:
  - *"The child doesn't want to go."*
  - *"The child says s/he can't stand him/her."*
  - *"The child feels uncomfortable around him/her."*
  - *"The child doesn't like the new stepparent/girl/boyfriend."*
- Encourages the child to refuse phone calls, ignore messages, or avoid visits despite prior positive relationships.

Chapter #16: Red Flags for Identifying an Alienating Parent

3. Encouraging the Child to Reject the Other Parent

- Uses phrases like:
    - *"It's your choice, but if you love me, you won't want to see him/her."*
    - *"If I were you, I wouldn't want to spend another moment in his/her presence."*
    - *"If I'd been made to feel the way he/she makes you feel, I wouldn't spend another second with him/her!"*
- The child starts using adult-like language or repeating words or legal accusations they could not have formed independently.

4. False Allegations Against the Other Parent

- Repeated accusations of abuse, neglect, or incompetence without evidence.
- The alienating parent seems to coach the child to make false claims in court or therapy.
- False allegations of abuse are a primary tool in severe parental alienation cases, often used to completely sever the relationship between the child and the targeted parent (Harman & Lorandos, 2021).

5. Emotional Manipulation and Guilt-Tripping

- The child is rewarded for rejecting the other parent via extra attention, gifts, privileges, etc.
- The alienating parent acts distressed or "betrayed" if the child expresses interest in seeing the targeted parent.
- Examples of what an alienating parent might say to a child:
    - *"If you go see your dad/mom, it will break my heart!"*
    - *"I love you more than he/she will ever love you!"*
    - *"Mommy/Daddy needs you baby!"*
    - *"Mommy/Daddy will miss you SO much while you're gone! I hope my heart doesn't break!"*

Chapter #16: Red Flags for Identifying an Alienating Parent

- ○ *"I hope mommy/daddy doesn't die of a broken heart before you get back!"*

6. Role Reversal – The Child Becomes the Parent's Emotional Confidant

- The child is exposed to inappropriate adult conflicts, such as financial or legal issues between the parents.
  - ○ For instance, the child might say *"If dad/mom would do his/her part then we could afford to pay the bills."*
- The alienating parent treats the child as their therapist, seeking validation for their anger toward the other parent.
- Alienated children are often burdened with the responsibility of ensuring a parent's happiness, often sacrificing their own emotional well-being in the process (Baker, 2007).

7. Erasing or Rewriting Family History

- The alienating parent denies or distorts past positive experiences between the child and the targeted parent.
  - ○ For example: A child who once adored their father suddenly insists, *"He never loved me, he was always mean to me."*
  - ○ *"I used to think mom/dad was a good person but now I know he/she isn't."*
- Family photos, gifts, or references to the alienated parent are removed or destroyed.

8. Lack of Genuine Concern for the Child's Well-Being

- The alienating parent prioritizes conflict over the child's mental health, rejecting therapy or mediation.

- If court-ordered reunification therapy is mandated, the parent actively sabotages the process by undermining the therapist or coaching the child to resist.
- In extreme cases, an alienating parent may reject professional help as biased, which only deepens the child's isolation and hinders their chances of recovery (Harman et al., 2018).

9. Polarized, Black-and-White Thinking

- The alienating parent paints themselves as the "good" parent and the other as entirely "bad" or unsafe.
- The child mirrors this narrative, refusing to acknowledge any positive memories with the alienated parent.
    - For Example: A child who once loved both parents suddenly insists, *"Mom/Dad is evil. I never want to see him/her again."*
    - *"I can't believe I fell for the lies mom/dad have told me all this time. I'm so glad mom/dad has let me know the truth about what a terrible person mom/dad really is."*

10. Third-Party Enablers & Social Reinforcement

- Extended family, new partners, friends, or even religious figures are recruited to reinforce the alienation (e.g., a grandparent telling the child that the other parent abandoned them).
- The alienating parent aligns professionals (e.g., teachers, doctors) against the other parent by providing misleading information.
- The alienating parent often reaches out to others to gain support and validate their narrative, extending the impact beyond the parent-child relationship (Lorandos et al., 2013).

Chapter #16: Red Flags for Identifying an Alienating Parent

Chapter #16: Red Flags for Identifying an Alienating Parent

Markers of High Conflict Divorce or Separation

As outlined in Lorandos et al., *Parental Alienation: The Handbook for Mental Health and Legal Professionals* (2013, p.11):

Parental alienation (PA) typically arises in a pathogenic environment—one characterized by intense conflict between parents. While the specific manifestations of high-conflict separation or divorce may vary, the following behaviors and external markers are commonly observed:

- **Verbal aggression:** Abusive language, threats of violence
- **Physical aggression:** Slamming doors, throwing objects, physically endangering one another
- **Domestic violence:** Either actual incidents or allegations of abuse
- **Child sexual abuse allegations:** Whether substantiated or not
- **Emotional endangerment:** The child is subjected to psychological harm
- **History of access denial:** One parent repeatedly prevents the child from seeing the other parent
- **Family dysfunction:** Issues such as substance abuse or severe psychological disorders
- **Child welfare involvement:** Agencies intervene due to concerns about the child's well-being
- **Frequent attorney changes:** The case sees multiple legal representatives over time
- **Excessive litigation:** Unusual frequency of court appearances
- **Prolonged legal battles:** The case takes an extended period to reach resolution
- **Extensive documentation:** High volumes of evidence, including diaries and affidavits, are collected

126

Chapter #17: Markers of High Conflict Divorce or Separation

10 Reasons

"Empirical evidence and clinical literature have consistently revealed that the greater the level of severity in parental alienation cases, the greater the likelihood that the child and rejected parent will not reconcile with or without traditional therapeutic approaches."

(Reay, 2015)

_____

As outlined in Reay (2015) *Family Reflections: A Promising Therapeutic Program Designed to Treat Severely Alienated Children and Their Family System*:

10 Reasons Traditional Therapy Fails Parental Alienation (PA) Families

1. **Counterintuitive Nature** – Parental alienation cases are highly counterintuitive, making it difficult for non-specialists to recognize and address the problem effectively.

2. **Severity-Based Treatment Differences** – The therapeutic approach required for severely alienated children is vastly different from that for mild or moderate cases.

3. **Therapist Misalignment** – Many therapists, lacking specialized training, inadvertently align with the alienating parent and the programmed child, worsening the problem—a phenomenon known as *third-party alienation*.

4. **Clinician Bias & Family Annihilation** – Some therapists side with the alienating parent and child, excluding the target parent and

reinforcing alienation. This bias can contribute to complete family breakdown.

5. **Inability to Differentiate False vs. True Abuse Allegations** – Untrained professionals struggle to distinguish between legitimate abuse claims and the false allegations often seen in severe PA cases.

6. **Personality Disorders & Malicious Intent** – Alienating parents making false abuse claims often exhibit traits of borderline, narcissistic, or paranoid personality disorders, or sociopathic tendencies.

7. **Resistance to Therapy** – In severe PA cases, the alienating parent and child are too entrenched in their delusions to respond to traditional therapy.

8. **Therapist Shopping** – Alienating parents often fire therapists who challenge their behavior and seek professionals who validate their distorted narratives (Harman et al., 2018).

9. **Lack of Motivation** – Both alienating parents and children resist therapy, actively undermining treatment efforts.

10. **Ineffective Intervention Strategies** – Traditional therapy fails to remove the child from the alienating parent's influence, leaving them exposed to continued manipulation outside of sessions.

Practical Tips for Target Parents

1. **Stay Emotionally Regulated**

   Avoid reacting with anger or defensiveness when the child rejects you. Respond with patience and understanding to model emotional stability (Warshak, 2010).

2. **Keep the Door Open**

   Consistently express your love and willingness to reconnect, even if the child is resistant. Let them know you will always be there for them (Warshak, 2010).

3. **Counteract False Narratives with Truth, Not Conflict**

   Gently correct misinformation without criticizing the alienating parent. Use phrases like, "I remember things differently," to avoid escalating conflict (Warshak, 2010).

4. **Use Therapeutic Communication Techniques**

   Validate the child's feelings while offering alternative perspectives. Ask open-ended questions instead of making accusations (Lorandos et al., 2013).

5. **Engage in Positive Shared Activities**

   Suggest enjoyable activities that previously bonded you and your child, like playing games, reading, or watching favorite movies (Warshak, 2010).

6. **Keep Updated Photo Albums Readily Available**

   Since alienating parents often erase or distort past memories, maintain accessible photo albums with positive memories of your time together. When possible, share them with your child as a way to reinforce real experiences and challenge false narratives (Warshak, 2010)

7. **Avoid Bad Mouthing the Alienating Parent**

    Speaking negatively about the alienating parent can intensify the child's loyalty conflict, so it's important to model respectful behavior instead (Warshak, 2010).

8. **Use Written and Digital Communication Wisely**

    If direct contact is limited, stay connected through letters, emails, or texts that express unconditional love without placing pressure—keep your messages warm, concise, and consistent (Warshak, 2010).

9. **Encourage Critical Thinking Skills**

    Ask questions that help the child analyze inconsistencies in the alienation narrative, such as, "What do you think makes a good parent?" (Warshak, 2010).

10. **Reaffirm Your Love Without Pressure**

    Remind your child that your love is unwavering, even if they are distant and avoid making them feel guilty for their behavior (Warshak, 2010).

11. **Utilize Professional Support**

    Work with a therapist experienced in parental alienation to reinforce reunification strategies and support your mental well-being (Lorandos et al., 2013).

12. **Document Alienating Behaviors**

    Document every instance where the alienating parent disrupts your relationship with your child, as this information may be valuable in future legal proceedings (Lorandos et al., 2013).

Best Practices for Documenting Parental Alienation for Court Proceedings:

Accurate and detailed documentation is essential when addressing parental alienation in court. Evidence-based practices suggest the following strategies:

1. **Record Denied Visitations**: Keep a detailed log of instances where visitation rights were obstructed or denied. Include dates, times, and descriptions of each occurrence. Such records can substantiate claims of alienation.

2. **Gather School and Medical Records**: Collect documentation from educational institutions and healthcare providers that may reveal behavioral patterns or health issues in the child correlating with alienation. These records can provide objective insights into the child's well-being.

3. **Document Communications**: Document all relevant communications, such as emails, text messages, and social media interactions, that reflect manipulative actions or attempts at alienation. This evidence can help reveal patterns of behavior that harm the parent-child relationship.

4. **Maintain a Detailed Journal**: Regularly update a journal with observations of the child's statements and behaviors, noting any indications of alienation. Include specifics about interactions, emotional responses, and any third-party observations.

5. **Seek Professional Evaluations**: Engage mental health professionals to assess the child's emotional and psychological state. Their expert evaluations can serve as critical evidence in court.

13. Ensure Professional Integrity:
Verifying Licenses and Ethical Standing

To safeguard your interests, it's crucial to verify the credentials and ethical standing of each professional involved in your case. Here's how you can proceed:

1. **License Verification**: Confirm that each professional holds a valid and current license to practice in your state. Most state licensing boards offer online tools for this purpose. For instance, to verify a therapist's license, you can use your state's licensing board's website.

2. **Ethics Violation Check**: Investigate whether any professionals have faced disciplinary actions or ethics violations. Many state boards provide online databases or resources to access this information.

3. **Contact State Ethics Boards**: If online information is insufficient, reach out directly to the relevant state ethics boards or professional regulatory agencies. They can provide detailed records of any disciplinary actions or ethical breaches associated with the professionals in question. The American Bar Association offers resources for the public to locate appropriate state agencies.

By diligently verifying licenses and checking for any ethical violations, you ensure that the professionals handling your case adhere to the highest standards of integrity and competence.

Chapter #19: Practical Tips for Target Parents

Barriers to Identifying & Reporting PM

As outlined in Baker et al., *Providing Parents with Advice About Alternatives to Psychological Maltreatment* (2021, pp. 93-116):

Psychological maltreatment (PM) often goes unrecognized and untreated, putting children, families, and society at risk.

A recent survey of more than 500 professionals in the field of child maltreatment revealed that many were unaware of the various forms of parental manipulation (PM). The study also uncovered a strong reluctance to report parents engaging in such behaviors to child protection services, even when there was clear evidence of harm, the conduct was severe, and the parents showed no willingness or ability to change (as cited in Baker et al., 2021).

A national survey found that 40% of mandated reporters fail to report every suspected case of maltreatment to child protection services (as cited in Finkelhor & Zellman, 1991). Similarly, **another study revealed that half of medical professionals acknowledged not reporting all suspected incidents** (as cited in Schweitzer et al., 2006). This trend of underreporting has also been documented among teachers (as cited in Levin, 1983) and school psychologists (as cited in Bryant, 2009), indicating that reluctance to report is a common issue across multiple mandated reporting fields.

Several factors contribute to the hesitation in reporting PM, including:

- Uncertainty about what constitutes "reasonable suspicion" (as cited in Berkowitz, 2008; Levi et al., 2015).

- Concerns about damaging the therapeutic or professional relationship with clients (as cited in Agatstein, 1989).
- Fears of breaching confidentiality (as cited in Alvarez et al., 2004).
- Emotional distress or discomfort experienced by the reporter after making a report (as cited in Bell & Singh, 2016).
- Mandated reporters often struggle when it comes to identifying and reporting psychological maltreatment (PM).
- PM is frequently seen as vague and poorly defined, making it harder to distinguish from poor parenting practices (as cited in Baker & Brassard, 2019).
- Many state laws require clear evidence of specific harm for PM to be recognized, adding to the complexity of reporting.
- The absence of a clear boundary between substandard parenting and PM can lead to greater tolerance for PM behaviors compared to other forms of abuse (as cited in Crenshaw et al., 1995; Hawkins & McCallum, 2001; Nayda, 2002).
- Some professionals believe that reporting PM to child protective services (CPS) may not be the most effective or appropriate response.
- Some professionals feel that families should be given a chance to correct the behavior before involving authorities.
- A general lack of confidence or unfavorable views toward child protection services also contributes to the reluctance to report (as cited in Alexander, 1990; Morris et al., 1985).

Mandated reporters—such as teachers, therapists, pediatricians, and home visitors—often have ongoing relationships with the families they would need to report. These professionals may prefer to address concerning behaviors within the context of their existing relationships, through continued support or communication.

Research shows many mandated reporters worry that reporting could:

Chapter #20: Barriers to Identifying & Reporting PM

- Harm the therapeutic or educational relationship.
- Negatively affect the child or family.
- Damage the home environment.
- Lead to retaliation against the reporter or child (as cited in Alvarez et al., 2004).

So, what professional barriers exist that are keeping child advocates from identifying and reporting psychological abuse?

Barriers identified in this study included:
- First, most respondents indicated that their formal education did not adequately prepare them to prevent psychological maltreatment (PM) or to respond effectively when such cases arose.
- Secondly, just 20% of professionals working in the child maltreatment field felt that their colleagues were sufficiently trained to address psychological maltreatment. Consequently, the majority did not see their peers as dependable resources for support or guidance in dealing with PM-related cases.

So, what can be done?

#1. More PM Education & Training to Identify & Respond Effectively

There is a distinct need to strengthen training at both undergraduate and graduate levels to ensure professionals are prepared to prevent psychological maltreatment (PM) and respond effectively when it arises. Academic programs focused on working with families should include thorough instruction on all types of child maltreatment—PM included—as well as clear guidance on how to identify signs and implement appropriate intervention strategies.

In the absence of updates to educational curricula, family service agencies can take proactive steps by providing comprehensive training and support to their staff—especially those working directly with both foster and biological parents. This training should focus on helping staff recognize signs of psychological maltreatment and equip them with practical strategies for engaging parents who may be displaying such harmful behaviors.

Studies show that inadequate preparation among staff to address parenting challenges contributes to job dissatisfaction—an ongoing concern that has been associated with high turnover rates within the child welfare system (as cited in Rycraft, 1994; Shim, 2010).

To address this, it is recommended that all child welfare staff receive:
- Ongoing refresher (booster) training.
- Consistent supervision focused on how to effectively intervene with families exhibiting poor parenting behaviors.

One effective approach to in-service training is the coaching model, where:
- Experts provide support and training across the organization.
- Coaches are knowledgeable about the specific organizational and community context, allowing them to tailor expert knowledge to fit the local setting (as cited in Allen et al., 2020).

A key element of this coach training approach is the parallel process:
- The respectful, strengths-based, and compassionate way coaches interact with staff serves as a model for how staff should engage with parents. In turn, this models for parents how to interact positively with their children.

- Many staff prefer a consultative, supportive coaching style over a directive, monitoring approach, making the coaching model more effective and well-received (as cited in Rycraft, 1994).

Given that most professionals report not receiving adequate training to prevent or respond to psychological maltreatment (PM), future training programs should include these core components:

- A clear definition of psychological maltreatment and the various ways it can appear, particularly in relation to different cultural backgrounds and developmental stages of childhood.
- Guidance on identifying when poor parenting crosses the line into psychological maltreatment and meets the criteria for mandatory reporting.
- A comprehensive and persuasive explanation of the severe, lasting impact of psychological maltreatment, ensuring it is acknowledged and addressed with the urgency it warrants.

Chapter #20: Barriers to Identifying & Reporting PM

Chapter #20: Barriers to Identifying & Reporting PM

References

Adverse childhood experiences (aces). RWJF. (2025).
https://www.rwjf.org/en/insights/collections/adverse-childhood-experiences.html

American Bar Association. (1996). *Standards of practice for lawyers representing children in custody cases*.
https://www.americanbar.org/content/dam/aba/administrative/child_law/repstandwhole.pdf

American professional society on the abuse of children. American Professional Society on the Abuse of Children (APSAC). (2025, February 27). https://apsac.org/

American Psychiatric Association. (2013). *Diagnostic and statistical manual of mental disorders (5th ed.)*. Washington, DC: Author.
https://archive.org/details/diagnosticstatis0005unse/mode/2up

Amy J.L. Baker, Phd: Parental alienation. Dr. Amy J.L.Baker. (2025).
https://www.amyjlbaker.com/

Baker, A.J.(Ed.). (2020). Parental alienation strategies. Retrieved from
https://www.amyjlbaker.com/parental-alienation-syndrome.html

Baker, A. J. L. (2007). *Adult children of parental alienation syndrome: Breaking the ties that bind*. W. W. Norton & Company.

Baker, A. J. L., & Darnall, D. (2006). Behaviors and Strategies Employed in Parental Alienation: A Survey of Parental Experiences. *Journal of Divorce & Remarriage, 45*(1–2), 97–124. https://doi.org/10.1300/J087v45n01_06

Baker, A. J. L., & Eichler, A. (2016). The linkage between parental alienation behaviors and child alienation. *Journal of Divorce & Remarriage*, 57(7), 475-484.
https://doi.org/10.1080/10502556.2016.1220285

Baker, A. J. L., & Verrocchio, M. C. (2016). Exposure to parental alienation and subsequent anxiety and depression in Italian adults. *American Journal of Family Therapy*, 44(5), 255-271. https://doi.org/10.1080/01926187.2016.1230480

Baker, A. J. L., & Verrocchio, M. C. (2015). Parental bonding and parental alienation as correlates of psychological maltreatment in adults in intact and non-intact families. *Journal of Child and Family Studies*, 24(10), 3047–3057.
https://doi.org/10.1007/s10826-014-0108-0

Baker, A. J. L., Brassard, M. R., & Rosenzweig, J. (2021). Psychological maltreatment: Definition and reporting barriers among American professionals in the field of child abuse. *Child abuse & neglect, 114*, 104941.
https://doi.org/10.1016/j.chiabu.2021.104941

Baker, A. J. L., Brassard, M. R., & Rosenzweig, J. F. (2021). Providing parents with advice about alternatives to psychological maltreatment: A survey of professionals in the field of child maltreatment. *Child Welfare*, 99(1), 93–116.

Balmer, S., Matthewson, M., & Haines, J. (2018). Parental alienation: Targeted parent perspective. *Australian Journal of Psychology*, 70(1), 91–99.
https://doi.org/10.1111/ajpy.12159

Bernet, W. (2020). *Parental Alienation: Science and Law*. Charles C Thomas.

Bernet, W., Baker, A. J. L., & Adkins, K. L. (2022). Definitions and terminology regarding child alignments, estrangement, and alienation: A survey of custody evaluators. *Journal of Forensic Sciences*, 67(1), 279–288. https://doi.org/10.1111/1556-4029.1486

Bernet, W., Gregory, N., Reay, K. M., & Rohner, R. P. (2018). An objective measure of splitting in parental alienation: The Parental Acceptance-Rejection Questionnaire. *Journal of Forensic Sciences*, 63(3), 776-783. https://doi.org/10.1111/1556-4029.13625

Boch-Galhau, W. V. (2018). Parental alienation (syndrome): A serious form of psychological child abuse. *Mental Health and Family Medicine*, 13, 725–739.

Chadwick, D. L., Alexander, R., Esernio-Jenssen, D., Giardino, A. P., & Thackeray, J. D. (2014). *Chadwick's child maltreatment: Physical abuse and neglect (4th ed., Vol. 1)*. STM Learning.

Chadwick, D. L., Giardino, A., Alexander, R., Thackeray, J., & Esernio-Jenssen, D. (2014). *Chadwick's child maltreatment: Sexual abuse and psychological maltreatment (4th ed., Vol. 2)*. STM Learning.

Colorado State University. (2019, November 4). Whether direct or indirect, parental alienation harms families. *ScienceDaily*. Retrieved March 13, 2025, from www.sciencedaily.com/releases/2019/11/191104144131.htm

Gardner, R. A. (1998). *The parental alienation syndrome: A guide for mental health and legal professionals* (2nd ed.). Creative Therapeutics.

Glaser D. (2011). How to deal with emotional abuse and neglect: further development of a conceptual framework (FRAMEA). *Child abuse & neglect*, 35(10), 866–875. https://doi.org/10.1016/j.chiabu.2011.08.002

Harman, Jennifer Jill, & Biringnen, Z. (2016). *Parents acting badly: How institutions and societies promote the alienation of children from their loving families*. CreateSpace.

Harman, J. J., & Lorandos, D. (2021). Allegations of family violence in court: How parental alienation affects judicial outcomes. *Psychology, Public Policy, and Law, 27*(2), 184–208. https://doi.org/10.1037/law0000301

Harman, J. J., Bernet, W., & Harman, J. (2019). Parental Alienation: The Blossoming of a Field of Study. *Current Directions in Psychological Science, 28*(2), 212-217. https://doi.org/10.1177/0963721419827271

Harman, J. J., Kruk, E., & Hines, D. A. (2018). Parental alienating behaviors: An unacknowledged form of family violence. *Psychological Bulletin*, 144(12), 1275–1299. https://doi.org/10.1037/bul0000175

Harman, J. J., Leder-Elder, S., & Biringen, Z. (2016). Prevalence of parental alienation drawn from a representative poll. *Children and Youth Services Review, 66*, 62–66. https://doi.org/10.1016/j.childyouth.2016.04.021

Harman, J. J., & Lorandos, D. (2021). Allegations of family violence in court: How parental alienation affects judicial outcomes. *Psychology, Public Policy, and Law, 27*(2), 184–208. https://doi.org/10.1037/law0000301

References

Harman, J. J., Warshak, R. A., Lorandos, D., & Florian, M. J. (2022). Developmental psychology and the scientific status of parental alienation. *Developmental Psychology, 58*(10), 1887–1911. https://doi.org/10.1037/dev0001404

Hart, S. N., Brassard, M. R., Baker, A. J. L., & Chiel, Z. A. (2017). Psychological maltreatment of children. In J. Conte & B. Klika (Eds.), *The APSAC handbook on child maltreatment* (4th ed., pp. 145-162). Sage Publications.

Janoski, S. (2025, January 30). *Mom allegedly gunned down estranged husband - then drove across state lines to shoot another ex and his new girlfriend: "she's a monster."* New York Post. https://nypost.com/2025/01/30/us-news/twisted-mom-allegedly-shot-two-exes-and-one-of-their-new-girlfriends-killing-two/

Knox, M. (2024, September 15). *My scheming ex-wife killed my gran & tried to frame me to win custody battle.* The Irish Sun. https://www.thesun.ie/fabulous/13816523/worst-ex-ever-eric-hill-rosa-mei-netflix-murder-plot/

Kraayeveld Family Law. (2024, August 7). *Murders of children highlight the intensity of custody disputes.* https://www.kraayeveld.com/blog/deaths-of-children-show-connection-between-domestic-violence-custody-disputes/

Lee-Maturana, S., Matthewson, M. L., & Dwan, C. (2020). Targeted parents surviving parental alienation: Consequences of the alienation and coping strategies. *Journal of Child and Family Studies, 29*(8), 2268–2280. https://doi.org/10.1007/s10826-020-01725-1

Lorandos, D., Bernet, W., & Sauber, S. R. (2013). *Parental alienation: The handbook for mental health and legal professionals.* Charles C Thomas Publisher.

Marsden, J., Saunders, L., & Harman, J. J. (2024). Pilot study of parental alienation items in the adverse childhood experiences scale. *Journal of Affective Disorders, 367,* 715–744. https://doi.org/10.1016/j.jad.2024.09.001

Morrison, S. L., & Ring, R. (2023). Reliability of the Five-Factor Model for determining parental alienation. *American Journal of Family Therapy, 51*(5), 580–598. https://doi.org/10.1080/01926187.2021.2021831

Pearl, P. (2015). Psychological abuse. In A. Giardina, L. Shaw, P. Speck, & E. Giardina (Eds.), *Recognition of child abuse for the mandated reporter* (4th ed., pp. 67-94). STM Learning, Inc.

Reay, K. M. (2015). Family reflections: A promising therapeutic program designed to treat severely alienated children and their family system. *American Journal of Family Therapy, 43*(2), 197–207. https://doi.org/10.1080/01926187.2015.1007769

Roma, P., Marchetti, D., Mazza, C., Ricci, E., Fontanesi, L., & Verrocchio, M. C. (2022). A comparison of MMPI-2 profiles between parental alienation cases and custody cases. *Journal of Child and Family Studies, 31*(5), 1196–1206. https://doi.org/10.1007/s10826-021-02076-1

Staff, P. (2024, November 1). *Celebrity News, exclusives, photos and videos.* People.com.https://people.com/cause-death-revealed-kansas-women-al

References

legedly-killed-members-gods-misfits-group-8738148

Vallance, S., & Silva, K. (2024, December 11). *Family remember "beautiful girl" as husband found guilty of murder.* ABC News. https://www.abc.net.au/news/2024-12-11/emil-petrov-found-guilty-of-murdering-cindy-crossthwaite/104712234

Verrocchio, M. C., Baker, A. J., & Bernet, W. (2016). Associations between Exposure to Alienating Behaviors, Anxiety, and Depression in an Italian Sample of Adults. *Journal of forensic sciences, 61*(3), 692–698. https://doi.org/10.1111/1556-4029.13046

Verrocchio, M. C., Baker, A. J. L., & Marchetti, D. (2017). Adult report of childhood exposure to parental alienation at different developmental time periods. *Journal of Family Therapy,* 40(4), 602–618. https://doi.org/10.1111/1467-6427.12192

Warshak, R. A. (2010). *Divorce poison: How to protect your family from bad-mouthing and brainwashing.* HarperCollins

Warshak, R. A. (2015). Ten parental alienation fallacies that compromise decisions in court and in therapy. *Professional Psychology: Research and Practice, 46*(4), 235–249. https://doi.org/10.1037/pro0000031

References

www.ingramcontent.com/pod-product-compliance
Lightning Source LLC
Chambersburg PA
CBHW081631040426
42449CB00014B/3260